INTERNATIONAL
Lighting
DESIGN

Published 1996 by Laurence King Publishing
an imprint of Calmann & King Ltd
71 Great Russell Street
London WC1B 3BN

A catalogue record for this book is available
from the British Library.

ISBN 1 85669 086 5

Designed by Michael Phillips,
Archetype

Printed in Hong Kong

INTERNATIONAL
Lighting DESIGN

Jeremy
Myerson

ASSISTANT EDITOR

Jennifer
Hudson

Laurence King

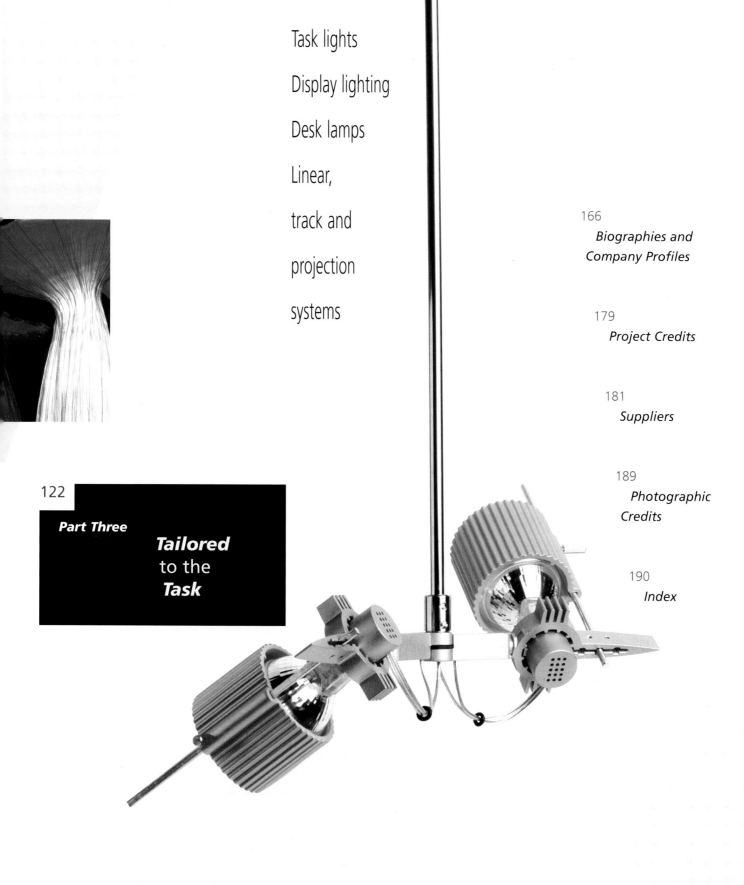

Task lights

Display lighting

Desk lamps

Linear,

track and

projection

systems

122

Part Three
Tailored
to the
Task

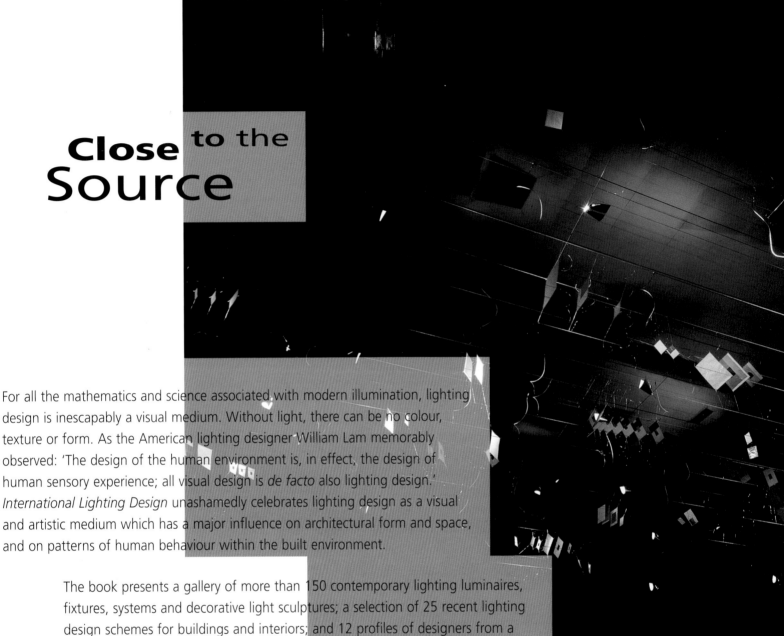

Close to the
Source

For all the mathematics and science associated with modern illumination, lighting design is inescapably a visual medium. Without light, there can be no colour, texture or form. As the American lighting designer William Lam memorably observed: 'The design of the human environment is, in effect, the design of human sensory experience; all visual design is *de facto* also lighting design.' *International Lighting Design* unashamedly celebrates lighting design as a visual and artistic medium which has a major influence on architectural form and space, and on patterns of human behaviour within the built environment.

The book presents a gallery of more than 150 contemporary lighting luminaires, fixtures, systems and decorative light sculptures; a selection of 25 recent lighting design schemes for buildings and interiors; and 12 profiles of designers from a variety of different backgrounds, including ceramics, fashion and architecture, who are developing new and alternative ideas in the field of lighting products. By focusing on the artistic and aesthetic potential of lighting, as opposed to the purely technical calculation of illumination, this publication seeks to unite within a single volume different facets of lighting design which are too often considered in isolation.

In particular I am referring to the traditional division between the world of light fitting or luminaire design – design of the instrument or fixture that directs and diffuses light – and the design of *light itself* within an architectural environment. Also, decorative light objects designed chiefly for domestic use rarely share the same pages as more technical lighting equipment for commercial or 'contract' interiors.

Ingo Maurer

Installation
YaYaHo ahaSoSo

for the 'Design and Identity'
exhibition (Louisiana Museum of Modern
Art, Humlebaek, Denmark, 1996)

Metal, plastic, multi-mirror reflectors, lacquered,
silver-plated and gold-plated square paper screens
Low-voltage halogen light source

There are historical reasons to explain why so many key strands in lighting design should have developed apart from each other. Lighting has occupied artists and designers for centuries. Long before the invention of electric light, architects studied the revelation of their buildings in sunlight and shadow, and poets, painters and sculptors eulogized about shooting stars, volcanoes, fireworks, rainbows and crimson sunsets, about the phenomenon of the naturally lit world. But it is only in the last 100 years that we have enjoyed the tools and technologies to produce and direct artificial light to our own design.

The first lighting designers of the modern era were the Art Nouveau glassware artists at the turn of the century. Louis Comfort Tiffany in America, and Emile Gallé and the Daum brothers in France instinctively understood the aesthetic importance of inventor Thomas Edison's successful development in 1879 of the world's first incandescent halogen light bulb – or lamp, as the lighting trade prefers to call it. These artists produced decorative stained-glass light fittings to incorporate electricity. Their glowing artefacts, with bases shaped like trees and shades in the form of butterfly wings or leaves, swiftly caught the public imagination. The age of gaslight and waxed candles was over.

So began the evolution of the modern electric light fitting, partly rooted in the decorative arts and partly rooted in industrial design, which continues to this day. It is a field that has advanced constantly, spurred on by technological development (primarily new materials and new light sources), social and economic change (the rise of a home-owning middle class) and aesthetic movements (from Art Deco and Machine Age themes to Post-Modernism).

At the beginning of the twentieth century, as the interiors of homes, hotels and clubs began to sport the first decorative electric light fittings, another entirely different form of lighting was developing in mines, tunnels, factories and offices – the outposts of industrialization – which enjoyed little or no design input. This lighting was strictly utilitarian, designed only to provide the most basic illumination with no aesthetic or sensory dimension. The German artist and

architect Peter Behrens is credited with producing the first utilitarian lights for
factories during his time as artistic director of the giant AEG industrial company
in Berlin in the years directly before World War One, but very soon such light
fittings were being designed anonymously and indiscriminately for mass
production.

So a pattern was set. More ornamental fittings and fixtures to direct and
diffuse light were in the hands of industrial designers, artists and, to a lesser
extent, architects (Charles Rennie Mackintosh and Josef Hoffmann both
designed light fittings for their buildings). The greater the formal and aesthetic
content of the light fitting, the greater the involvement of the designer. But
purely functional light tools for, say, factories were given little design
consideration as artefacts, and *application* of light within commercial spaces
became the exclusive province of electrical engineers who calculated light levels
using rigid scientific formulae and excluded more subjective criteria based on the
senses. Even those architects who fretted endlessly about the effects of natural
light on their building would tamely surrender the decision-making on use of
artificial light to scientists and engineers, with their charts and light-meters at the
ready. The result was much bland and indiscriminate application of light. This
trend was exacerbated by the invention of the fluorescent tube at General
Electric in America in the 1930s.

It was not until a pioneering group of stage lighting designers in America in the
1940s and 1950s began to take their skills outside the theatre into public and
commercial spaces that artificial lighting was given any real artistic consideration
in architecture. The work of Abe Feder, today the grand old man of American
lighting design, proved to be as significant in achieving a breakthrough in lighting
design as Tiffany had been earlier in the design of light fittings. Feder lit the New
York opening of *My Fair Lady* and the Orson Welles production of *Dr Faustus*, but
significantly he moved beyond the playhouse to design, amongst other things,
the lighting for the Rockefeller Center in New York, the *Queen Mary* ocean liner
and public plazas in Atlanta.

Hagia Sophia
Istanbul, Turkey

Erco Lighting
in co-operation with
Total Aydinlatma Mümessillik,
Istanbul.

A marble ritual vessel on the main
floor of this historic place of worship
is illuminated from an upper gallery by
pairs of Eclipse spotlights.

Feder and his peers brought the creative techniques of theatre, in which lighting design complements sets and costumes and underwrites the artistic intent of the production, to building and interior design. Their work established a new architectural lighting movement which prepared the ground for the current generation of international lighting consultants, many of whom trained first in stage lighting. The American tradition in lighting design, which emerged from the theatre, regarded lighting in terms of what you could see, not what you could measure. The message was that you should not trust light-meters, you should only trust your own eyes.

Analysis of the lighting schemes selected for *International Lighting Design* will confirm both the theatrical heritage and the current vibrancy of American lighting design. Many of the chosen projects are winners of the International Association of Lighting Designers (IALD) Awards, the most prestigious awards scheme in the United States. Paul Gregory's spectacular colour-changing design for the Entel Tower in Chile (featured on page 110), Paul Marantz's richly seductive scheme for the Mexican Gallery in the British Museum (page 148), and Ross De Alessi's sensitive treatment of the Santa Barbara County Courthouse (page 164) all demonstrate an indefinably creative intuition allied to technical mastery of light source and luminaire technology. Paul Gregory trained and worked first in the theatre, as did UK consultant Andre Tammes, whose firm Lighting Design Partnership is represented in this volume by an innovative scheme to light a pedestrian walkway at Manchester Airport (page 162). 'You have to learn to trust the intuitive process as a lighting designer,' says Tammes. 'Light doesn't exist until it strikes something, so lighting designers have to be concerned with the colour and texture and form of the physical materials the light strikes, not just with the lighting equipment. There is a duality to the thinking.'

Many of the lighting schemes in *International Lighting Design* deal with the problems of combining artificial light and daylight. Others are intricately bound up in building restoration. All subscribe to the philosophy outlined by the nineteenth-century stage designer and prophet of modern lighting design technique, Adolphe Appia, who said: 'Shade and shadow are equal in importance to light

itself'. But if some of the finest lighting schemes *per se* have their origins in the mature lighting practices of the United States, it is Europe and Japan that are setting the pace in luminaire or light fitting design. In some cases, the products being developed by such talents as Germany's Ingo Maurer or Japan's Kazuko Fujie are so ambitious in conception that they bridge the divide between luminaire design and lighting design. Maurer's lighting for Ron Arad's foyer areas in the new Tel Aviv Opera House and for the Louisiana Museum in Copenhagen, and Fujie's *Flying Lights* for a bridge in Kumamoto City, belong to a hybrid category of lighting installations in space which work on two levels – as art objects in their own right and as instruments that create light quality within an environment.

Maurer in particular is adamant that maximum light effect should be achieved with minimal effort, and he argues that many current lighting projects go to extremes in terms of utilizing the technology available: 'I don't mind architectural jewels being lit up,' he says, 'but large corporate offices on the way to the airport are lit like castles and I don't like it!' Maurer's work over the past 30 years has been a personal expression of beauty and poetry in light, whilst constantly utilizing technological advances, especially in light sources. Other designers, too, from a variety of disciplines, regard the light fitting as a suitable vehicle for individual creative experiment. What French fashion designer Jean-Charles de Castelbajac describes as the 'natural eloquence' of lighting has been a magnet drawing every type of designer to the challenge of the luminaire. The result, as this volume shows, is a wealth of creativity in a variety of media – from the glowing bone china of Japanese ceramicist Masatoshi Sakaegi to the organic crushed silk forms of Israeli fine artist Ayala Sperling-Serfaty and the ensemble of frosted polycarbonate by Barcelona-based architect Jorge Pensi.

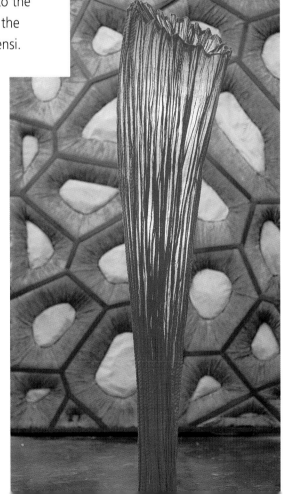

Ayala
Sperling-Serfaty

Standard lamp
Mermaid
Metal, silk
h 160cm di 35cm
h 63in di 13¾in
Limited batch production
Manufacturer Aqua
Israel

Ingo
Maurer
Ribbon of Gold

designed for the Tel Aviv Opera
Inauguration, October 1994

Gold-plated aluminium
230w halogen bulb
l 800cm drop 500cm
l 315in drop 196⅞in
One-off

Some of the lighting products in this volume belong to the utilitarian tradition of fitness for purpose in lighting. They are increasingly discreet and compact, in response to the progressive miniaturization of light-source technology; they emphasize energy efficiency and they perform their task unobtrusively. Other luminaires are overtly fun or iconic objects – limited edition lighting artefacts bearing the often idiosyncratic signature of their designer, whether it be the Villiers Brothers, Katrien Van Liefferinge or Weyers and Borms.

However, the line between style-led and function-led lighting has been increasingly blurred since workplace lighting forms such as track-lighting and spotlights entered the home, and influential manufacturers such as Flos of Italy began to promote an industrial-chic look in the 1960s. Some fittings in my selection belong to both camps in that they are conspicuously fit for their purpose whilst making a strong visual statement as objects. Danish designer Knud Holscher's *Zenit* uplighter for Erco, for example, is a precision office uplighter with an intriguing wing-like profile; Isao Hosoe's desk light is shaped like and named after a heron (see page 125). These are, in the words of industrial designers Perry King and Santiago Miranda, 'soft tools'. King Miranda's engaging new work for Sirrah (page 20) and Louis Poulsen (page 135) subscribes to this dual philosophy.

Hartmut S. Engel

Spot system
Dancer 33
Die-cast aluminium, polycarbonate, plastic
Max. 100w 240v tungsten halogen bulbs
Various sizes
Manufacturer
Staff, Germany

All of these cross-currents in lighting are expressed within a simple editorial structure for *International Lighting Design* which unites products, people and projects in three main sections. 'The Architecture of Light' discusses luminaires which are an essential part of the architectural fabric, alongside lighting schemes which effectively define the architectural experience. 'The Art of the Decorative' takes us into the realms of beauty, fantasy and design imagination, both in terms of the light specials, sculptures and

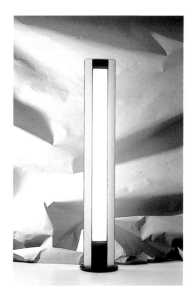

Hartmut S.
Engel

Standard lamp
Spheros
2 x 58w fluorescents,
2 x 50w tungsten halogen bulbs
h 184.2cm di 35cm
h 72in di 13⅞in
Manufacturer
Zumtobel Staff, Austria

Knud
Holscher

Standard lamp
Zenit
Aluminium, frosted glass
70/150/250w halogen bulb
h 185cm di 25.2cm
h 72⅞in di 9⅞in
Manufacturer
Erco Leuchten GmbH, Germany

chandeliers featured, and the colourful and decorative ways in which light can be applied to buildings. Finally, 'Tailored to the Task' embodies the idea of lighting being fit for a special purpose – whether the task in hand is to light a desk or the exterior of a famous architectural landmark.

Internationally, lighting has never been at a more exciting stage in its development. Technology is advancing all the time, with ever more sophisticated controls. Perception of the role of lighting consultants on the building design team is growing too. Nowadays no major hotel or shopping centre in Europe or America is built without prior recourse to lighting design expertise. Meanwhile, the single lighting object – elusive, sculptural, containing that magic ingredient of light – remains a compelling creative challenge for many artists and designers. Lighting may be part-art and part-science, but at the heart of all current activity is the essentially visual nature of the medium, which communicates first and foremost on an entirely emotional and sensory level.

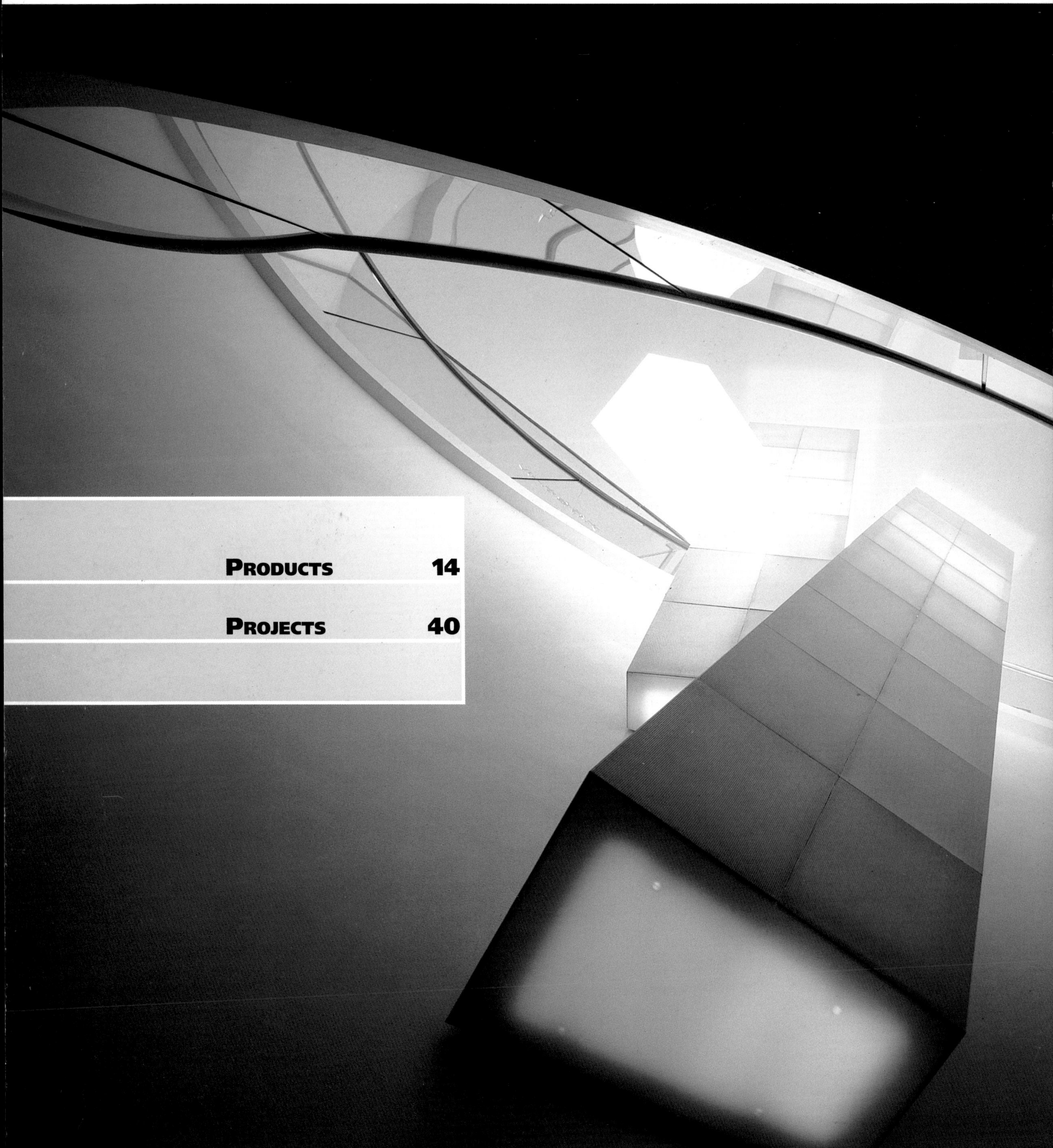

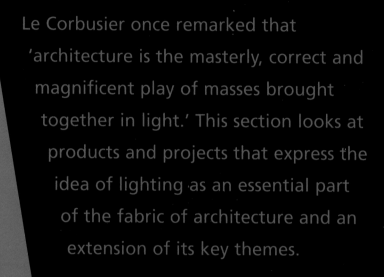

The
Architecture of
Light

Le Corbusier once remarked that 'architecture is the masterly, correct and magnificent play of masses brought together in light.' This section looks at products and projects that express the idea of lighting as an essential part of the fabric of architecture and an extension of its key themes.

The downlights, uplighting, wall, floor and ceiling lights, spotlights and systems shown here enhance and underscore the design intent of buildings and interiors – from the innovative modular systems of German duo Feldmann & Schultchen to the Baldinger products of leading American architect Richard Meier.

The designers of light fittings

who are profiled in this section express the belief that light solutions should be related to spatial concepts: King Miranda's poetic material invention with lighting for Sirrah, for example, mirrors the duo's own exploration of unusual surface finish in interior projects, while Kazuko Fujie's unique light structures are magnificent installations spanning architectural space.

Finally, the selection of projects shows examples in which the lighting design essentially defines the architectural experience – from the British Airways Compass Centre at Heathrow Airport to the restoration of the awe-inspiring Hagia Sophia church in Istanbul.

3

2

2

Torsten
Neeland

Suspension light
Lawrence
Metal, chrome, opaque glass
20w high-voltage energy-saving bulb
l 160–220cm di 10cm
l 63–86⅝in di 3⅞in
Manufacturer
ANTA, Germany

3

Torsten
Neeland

Standard lamp
Jeremy
Metal, chrome, opaque glass
100w high-voltage bulb
h 180cm di 26cm
h 70⅞in di 10¼in
Manufacturer
ANTA, Germany

1
(pages 14-15)

Kazuko
Fujie

Staircase lighting cluster
Moment-e
Perforated steel, acrylic
400w HID bulb
h 600cm w 204cm d 150cm
h 236¼in w 80⅜in d 59in
One-off
Manufacturer
Daiko, Japan

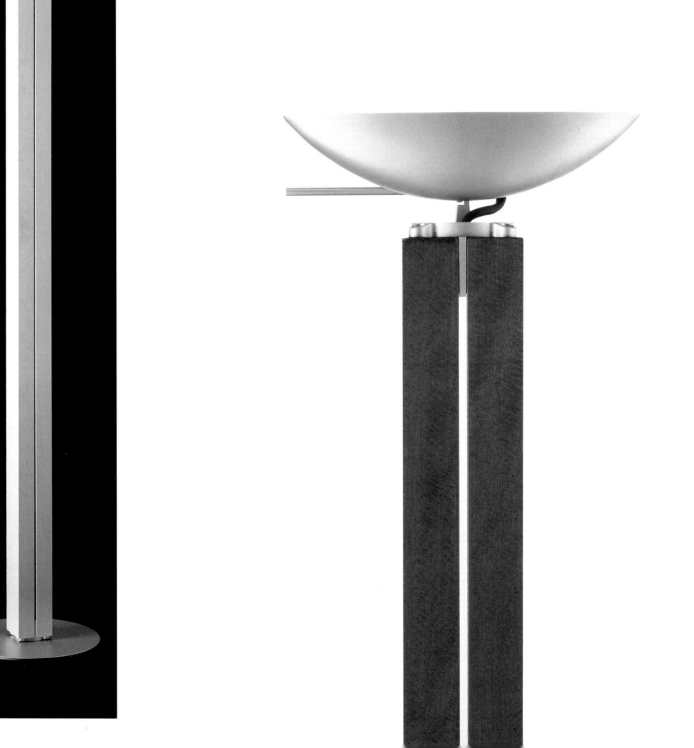

4

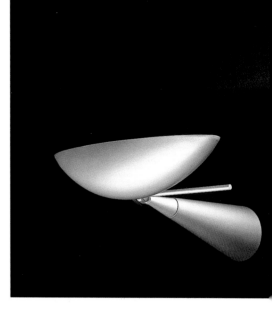

4

Sigeaki Asahara

Series of lights
Mehnir
Enamelled die-cast aluminium, wood or moulded
thermoplastic
300w bulb
Wall light: h 12.5cm d 25.5cm
h 4⅞in d 10in
Standard lamp: h 185cm di 34cm
h 72⅞in di 13⅜in
Manufacturer
Lucitalia SpA, Italy

5

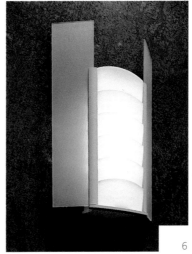

6

5

6

Perry A.
King

and Santiago
Miranda

Series of lights
Tina
Metal
300w halogen bulb
Wall light: h 38cm w 23cm d 16cm
h 15in w 9in d 6⅜in
Standard lamp: h 185cm di 28cm
h 72⅜in di 11in
Manufacturer
   Sirrah srl gruppo i Guzzini, Italy

Perry A.
King

and Santiago
Miranda

Series of lights
Aries
Plastic, glass, metals
Fluorescent
Wall light: h 33.5–55cm w 29cm d 10cm
h 13⅛ –21⅝in w 11⅜in d 3⅞in
Suspension light: h 12cm w 29cm l 153cm
h 4¾in w 11⅜in l 60¼in
Manufacturer
   Flight (division of Flos SpA), Italy

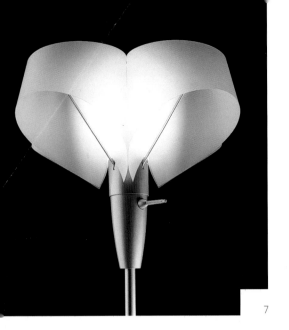

7

Perry A.
King
and Santiago
Miranda

Standard lamp
Mr Collar
Polycarbonate, glass fibre, nylon
150w frosted halogen bulb
Standard lamp: h 190cm di 28cm
h 74¾in di 11in
Manufacturer
Sirrah srl gruppo i Guzzini, Italy

7

9

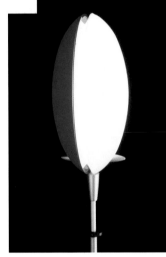

8

8

Perry A.
King
and Santiago
Miranda

Ceiling light
CCP1
Opaline methacrylate plates
32w fluorescent/100w bulb
h 27–31cm di 50cm
h 10⅝–12¼in di 19⅝in
Manufacturer
Sirrah srl gruppo i Guzzini, Italy

9

Perry A.
King
and Santiago
Miranda

Series of lights
MoM
Methacrylate
100w E27 or 36w 2G10 fluorescent
Standard lamp: h 140–180cm di 28cm
h 55⅛–70⅞in di 11in
Table lamp: h 60cm di 22cm
h 23⅝in di 8⅝in
Manufacturer
Sirrah srl gruppo i Guzzini, Italy

Profile

King Miranda

For British industrial designer Perry King and his Spanish partner Santiago Miranda, a new chapter has opened in lighting design. Their long-term relationship with Italian manufacturer Flos–Arteluce, which stretched back to the mid-1970s and included such classics as the *Jill* uplighter, ended in 1993. Today the Milan-based duo are working with Sirrah, part of the Guzzini group. This company has a distinguished record in lighting (Man Ray once designed a light for Sirrah) and plans to expand in the domestic market. The new collection of Sirrah products shown here reflects King Miranda's interest in using new materials to create 'emotion in lighting'. The design team that gave us lights made of fabric and Velcro for the 1992 Barcelona Olympics is now working with the diffusing qualities of glass-fibre-reinforced polycarbonate and methacrylate for Sirrah.

King Miranda are well-versed in designing a wide range of artefacts, from chairs to computers. Yet lighting remains a constant theme. 'We are so interested because lighting sets several problems,' says Miranda. 'It is about function, safety, technology, energy saving. But it remains an emotional project. In our lights, technology is never dominant. We're interested in soft tools.'

One Sirrah product, the *CCP 1* ceiling light, comprises a core of 24 thin white opaline methacrylate plates in a design subtly reminiscent of Poul Henningsen's classic 1950s work for the Scandinavian manufacturer Louis Poulsen. So there is an interesting twist to the news that King and Miranda have been chosen by Louis Poulsen to design new light fittings. Certainly, as designers who always try to express the poetic in functional objects, they are worthy successors to Henningsen. Perry King is an admirer of Scandinavian lighting: 'Drive into Milan and you see hard, white light. Drive into Copenhagen and you see soft, coloured light. You feel the Scandinavians would still like to be using candles.' The first Poulsen product by King Miranda is an outdoor bollard (see page 135). Meanwhile the Sirrah programme continues apace, with the *Tina 2* standard lamp perhaps most expressive of the duo's philosophy of giving lighting tools a more emotional dimension. A halogen bulb directs a hard white light up to the ceiling, but seven portholes in the fitting reveal the soft coloured light of a filter in a way which, says Perry King with evident satisfaction, 'makes a nonsense of functionalism'.

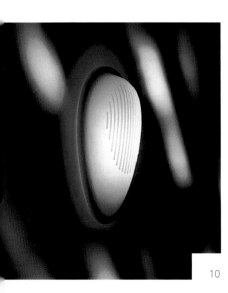

10

10

Marc
Sadler

Wall or ceiling light
Drop 1
Opalescent silicone elastomer, engineering polymer
9w fluorescent bulb
h 8.5cm w 12.7cm l 24.6cm
h 3⅜in w 5in l 9⅝in
Manufacturer
        Arteluce Div. Flos SpA, Italy

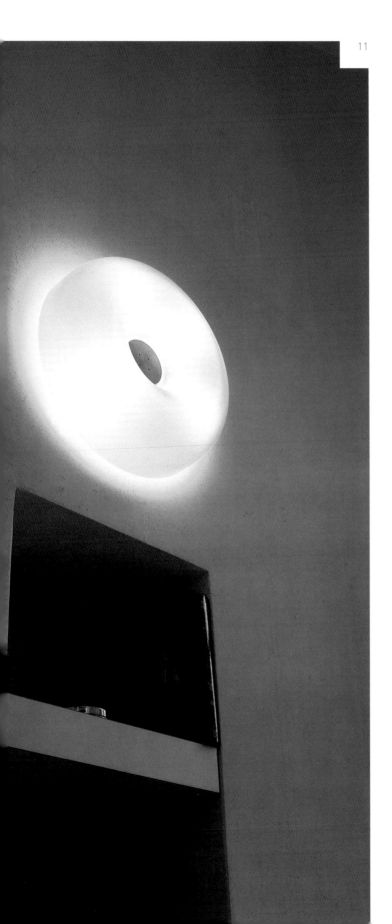

11

12

11

Defne
Koz

Wall light
Circus
Glass, metal
4 x 40w incandescent bulbs
d 11cm di 32cm
d 4 ⅜ in di 12 ⅝ in
Manufacturer
Foscarini, Italy

12

Jose Martí
Garcia

Wall light
Teso
Bubinga wood, brass, chrome
220v halogen bulb
h 87cm w 37cm d 25–100cm
h 34 ¼ in w 15 ⅛ in d 9 ⅞–39 ⅜ in
Manufacturer
Antonio Almerich SL, Spain

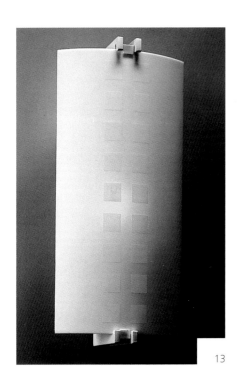

13

13

**Richard
Meier**

Wall sconce
Ana
Glass, metal
Incandescent or fluorescent bulb
h 32cm w 15cm d 10cm
h 12 ¾ in w 6in d 4in
Manufacturer
Baldinger Architectural Lighting, USA

14

**Philippe
Starck**

Wall light
Wall.A Wall.A
Technopolymer plastic, opaline plastic
9w compact fluorescent bulb
h 37cm w 30cm d 10cm
h 14 ½ in w 11 ⅞ in d 4in
Manufacturer
Flos SpA, Italy

15

15

Maurizio
Peregalli

Series of lights
Musina
Steel, ceramic
100w bulb
Standard lamp: h 170cm w 15cm l 15cm
h 66⅞in w 5⅞in l 5⅞in
Wall light: h 26cm w 10cm l 9cm
h 10¼in w 3⅞in l 3½in
Manufacturer
　　　Noto-Zeus, Italy

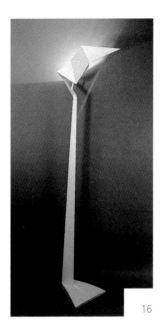

16

Kazuko
Fujie

Series of lights
Mangekyo
Perforated steel
65w halogen bulb
Wall uplighter: h 34cm w 15cm l 33cm
h 13⅜in w 5⅞in l 13in
Table lamp: h 40cm w 19cm l 65cm
h 15¾in w 5⅞in l 25⅜in
Standard lamp: h 182cm w 36cm l 56cm
h 71⅛in w 14⅛in l 22in
Limited batch production
Manufacturer
　　　Daiko, Japan

16

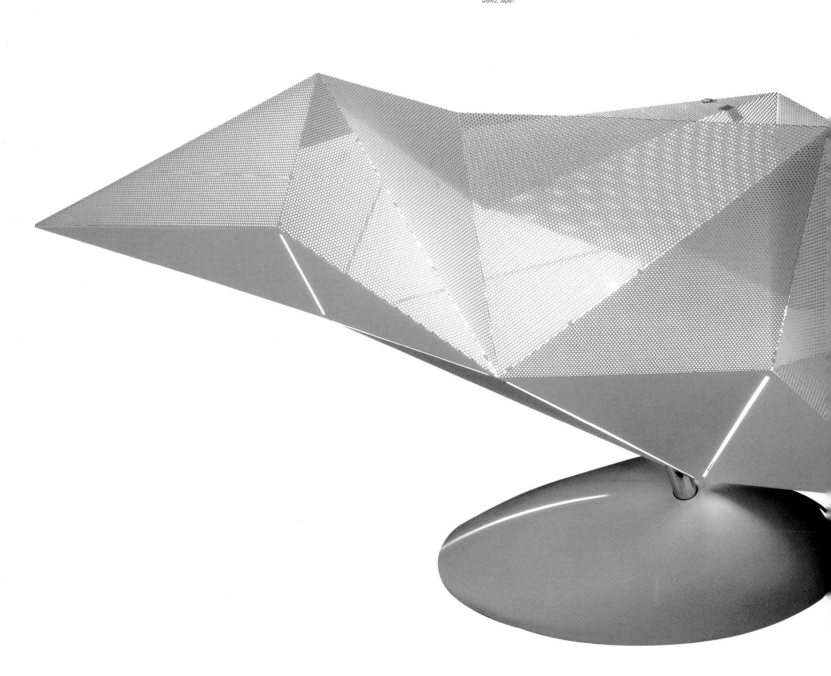

Profile

Kazuko **Fujie**

Kazuko Fujie is one of the most innovative lighting designers at work in Japan today. Her special interest is design for public spaces, from theatre lobbies to bridges. It is a focus that reflects her background. After graduating from Musashino Fine Arts University, she worked for the Miyawaki architectural practice and Endo Planning before setting up her own design office in 1987.

'I started work in a building design office and gained a lot of experience working with architects,' she recalls. 'I became particularly interested in using light and design to improve the quality of public spaces.'

She first attracted international attention a couple of years ago when her *Flying Lights* appeared on one of the bridges across the River Shirakawa in the centre of Kumamoto City in southern Japan (see page 54). Rather than propose conventional 'catalogue' street lights, she developed a design scheme based on a series of characterful structures made up of different triangular shapes. At night, a diversity of shining lights and reflections glitter

on the river. By day, the lights appear as a unique roof over the pavements and cast patterned shadows on the ground. 'Bridges in Japan are still very functional and similar in appearance. Yet people's views of a city can be romantically and nostalgically focused on bridges,' says Kazuko Fujie.

The *Flying Lights* project led directly to a commission from Japanese manufacturer Daiko to design a series of light fittings for domestic use, called *Mangekyo*, based on a very similar theme of irregular triangular planes of painted steel. There are three types in the range: wall uplighter, table lamp and floor uplighter. Although this work was an unusual departure for Fujie who normally works on a far larger scale, it reflected her interest in achieving visual and spatial quality through an architecture of light.

This fascination is perhaps best expressed through a further collaboration with Daiko on a project to create large-scale lighting for a spiral staircase leading down to a basement Tokyo theatre. Entitled *Moment*, Fujie's solution in coloured perforated steel and white acrylic creates a neutral, abstract space suffused with soft, gentle light between the ground-floor level and the auditorium below (see page 14). Its form consists of translucent cuboids distorted to exaggerate the perspective from the lower level. Fujie's most ambitious work occupies a kind of middle ground between the light instrument and light as a definer of architectural space. It is a unique approach enhanced by a sculptural quality.

16

19

17

17
Massimo
Sacconi

Ceiling light
Trottola
Aluminium, glass, polycarbonate
32 + 40w neon bulbs, 1 x E27 bulb
h 20cm di 55cm
h 7⅞in di 21⅝in
Manufacturer
Nordlight SpA, Italy

18
Box Design &
Products

Uplighter for
Hôtel du Département,
Marseilles
Mild steel, epoxy polyester
55w fluorescent bulb
h 13.5cm w 60cm d 33cm
h 5⅜in w 23⅝in d 13in
One-off
Manufacturer
Concord Sylvania Specials
Department, UK

20

18

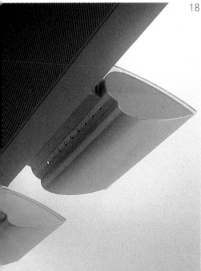

21

21
Richard
Meier

Pendant
Joseph
Glass, metal
Incandescent or fluorescent bulb
w 53.5cm d 122cm
w 21in d 48in
Manufacturer
Baldinger Architectural Lighting, USA

22
Sergio
Calatroni

Ceiling/wall light
Cardium Grande
Bronze
150w bulb
h 130cm w 12cm l 8cm
h 51¼in w 4¾in l 3⅛in
Limited batch production
Manufacturer
Afro City Edition, Italy

19
Concord
Sylvania/

Julian
Powell-Tuck

Downlight
LED 100
Diecast aluminium
10/13/18w bulbs
d 9.5cm di 18.5cm
d 3¾in di 7½in
Manufacturer
Concord Sylvania, UK

20
Philippe
Starck

Suspension light
Romeo Moon
Steel wire, moulded glass
150w incandescent bulb
h 22.5cm di 50cm
h 8⅞in di 19⅝in
Manufacturer
Flos SpA, Italy

22

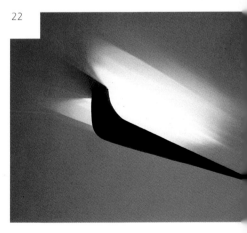

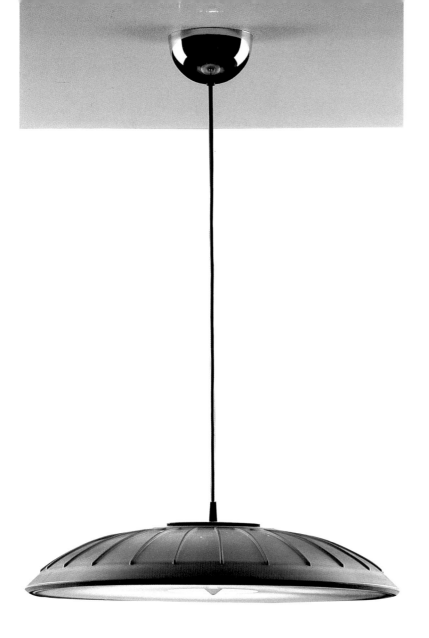

23

Novell/
Puig Design

Series of lights
Morris
Recycled almond shell, opal methacrylate
32w fluorescent (suspension), 13w bulb (wall),
23w compact fluorescent (ceiling & floor)
Suspension light: h 156cm di 50cm
h 61⅜in di 19⅝in
Wall light: h 17cm w 26–78cm d 7cm
h 6⅝in w 10¼–30¾in d 2¾in
Manufacturer
Vanlux SA, Spain

24

24

25

24

**Feldmann
& Schultchen**

Helix
Aluminium, plastic
26w 220v energy-saving bulb
h 55cm w 55cm l 160cm
h 21⅝in w 21⅝in l 63in
Prototype
Manufacturer
        Feldmann & Schultchen, Germany

25

**Feldmann &
Schultchen**

Lighting system
Fensterlicht
Glass, steel
26w 220v bulb, energy-saving tube bulbs
w 25cm l 200cm d 20cm
w 9⅞in l 78¾in d 7⅞in
Prototype
Manufacturer
        Feldmann & Schultchen, Germany

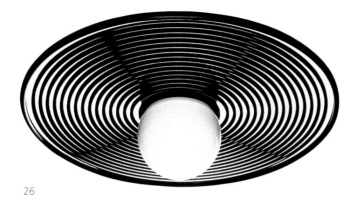

26

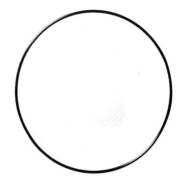

26

Franco
Bettonica

and Mario
Melocchi

Ceiling light
Diska
Polyamide, mirror glass
Max. 150w bulb
h 8.4cm di 36.5cm
h 3¼in di 14½in
Manufacturer
Cini & Nils, Italy

27

Franco
Bettonica

and Mario
Melocchi

Standard lamp
Mixa
Transparent crystal, steel, aluminium
Max. 500w bulb
h 198cm di 35.4cm
h 78in di 14in
Manufacturer
Cini & Nils, Italy

27

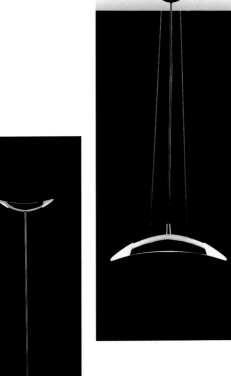

29

Jorge *Pensi*

Series of lights
Horus
Polished aluminium, glass
300w halogen bulb (standard), 150w linear
halogen bulb (suspension)
Standard lamp: h 188cm di 25cm
h 74in di 9⅞in
Suspension light: w 40cm l max. 160cm
w 15¾in l max. 63in
Manufacturer
    B. Lux SA, Spain

29

28

30

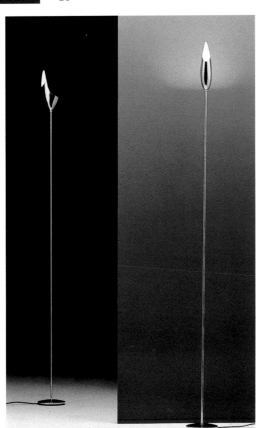

28

Jorge *Pensi*

Series of lights
Adar
Polished aluminium, sanded glass
150w halogen bulb
Standard lamp: h 195cm di 17cm
h 76¾in di 6¾in
Wall light: h 20cm d 21cm
h 7⅞in d 8¼in
Manufacturer
    B. Lux SA, Spain

30

Jorge *Pensi*

Series of lights,
Lobby
Polycarbonate, aluminium
40w incandescent bulbs
Set 1–7: h 16cm d 15.5cm l 20–80cm
h 6⅛in d 6⅛in l 7⅞–31½in
Suspension light: w 45cm l 100cm
w 17¾in l 39⅜in
Manufacturer
    Vanlux SA, Spain

Profile

Jorge Pensi

Jorge Pensi has been described as representing the flair and ingenuity of Spanish design without actually being Spanish. He is in fact Argentinian and he trained originally as an architect. Today, however, he is regarded as one of Barcelona's finest furniture designers. Pensi's aluminium *Toledo* restaurant chair, designed for Amat, became one of the most popular designs of the late 1980s and today adorns café pavements all over Europe. Yet this prolific designer also has a strong track record in lighting. All his work is for the same Spanish manufacturer, B. Lux and its sister company V. Lux, and dates back to 1984.

'My interest in lighting stems from the fact that the light fitting is two objects,' explains Pensi. 'When it is switched off, it is a symbolic object. When switched on, it is a functional tool to give light.' He also makes a distinction between 'lighting for architects who are looking for something more neutral' and 'lighting for interior designers who want something more symbolic'.

Pensi's instincts are increasingly towards the architectural: he is currently working with B. Lux on an 'Archilight' programme of fittings which will be installed in buildings as part of their essential fabric before the interior fit-out. However, much of his work has successfully courted the interior design market due to its sculptural grace and invention with materials. Pensi's flexible *Lobby* series, for example, is based on the idea of an ensemble of 'frosted' polycarbonate diffusers attached to polished aluminium hangers on an extruded aluminium rail. 'The idea of a rail for lights on a wall came from looking in restaurants. *Lobby* is a low-cost solution which enables many different combinations. You can take the lights from the wall, clean and replace them without screws.'

Pensi points out that while materials may sometimes be included in the B. Lux brief, the basic design concept never is. That is where he comes into his own, as a creative mind constantly alert to the potential of new forms and directions. The majority of his Spanish clients are to be found in the Basque Country, but Pensi and his three studio collaborators also work much further afield: in Germany, Italy, Korea, Singapore and South America. 'I work all the time and I'm fast,' laughs Pensi, but behind the gentle smile is a design portfolio which suggests that no corners are cut in getting it right.

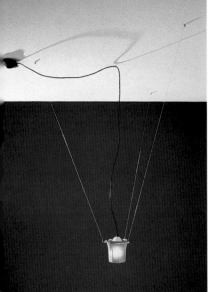

31

32

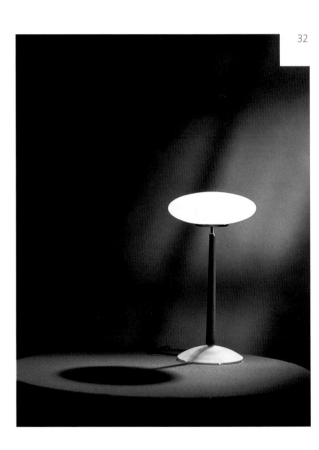

31

Lluis **Clotet**

Suspension light
Polux
Brass, sanded glass, steel
100w 220v bulb
h 17.5cm di 15cm
h 6⅞in di 5⅞in
Manufacturer
Bd. Ediciones de Diseño SA, Spain

32

Matteo Thun

Table lamp
PAO T1
Etched blown glass, cherrywood
35w 12v bulb
h 33.5cm di 19.6cm
h 13 ¼ in di 7 ¾ in
Manufacturer
    Flos SpA, Italy

33

Matteo Thun

Standard lamp
PAO F
Etched blown glass, cherrywood
300w linear halogen bulb
h 191cm di 37cm
h 75 ¼ in di 14 ⅝ in
Manufacturer
    Flos SpA, Italy

32

33

34

34

Carlo Bartoli

Standard lamp
Calice
Recyclable Baydur, metal
250w bulb
h 183cm di 30cm
h 72in di 11⅞ in
Manufacturer
    Antonangeli Illuminazione srl, Italy

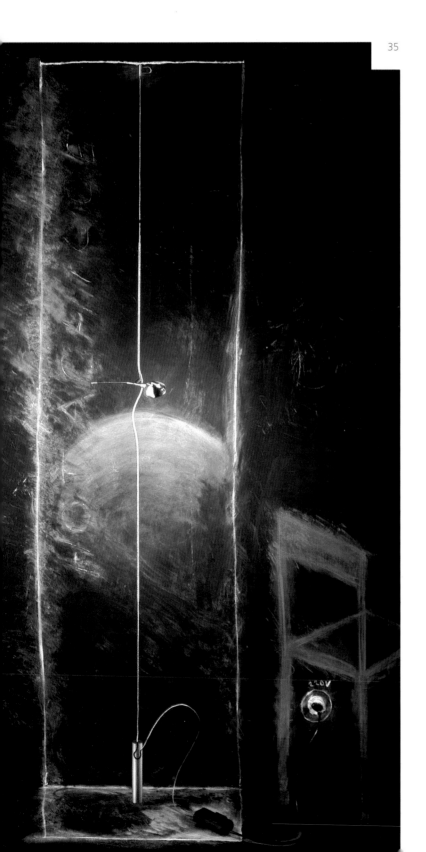

35

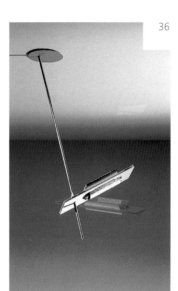

35

Ingo
Maurer

Floor to ceiling light
Hot Achille
Aluminium, stainless steel
50w bulb
h adjustable by up to 100cm
h adjustable by up to 39½ in
Limited batch production
Manufacturer
Ingo Maurer GmbH, Germany

36

Ingo
Maurer

Ceiling light
Wandering Finger
Stainless steel, anodized aluminium,
heat-resistant glass
150w 230/125v halogen bulb
h 45cm w 24cm
h 17¾ in w 9⅜ in
Manufacturer
Ingo Maurer GmbH, Germany

37

Bernhard
Dessecker,
Ingo
Maurer
and team

Pendant,
Lucetto
Transparent plastic, heat-resistant shade
75w 230/125v PAR 30 flood
h 21cm di 28cm
h 8½ in di 11 in
Manufacturer
Ingo Maurer GmbH, Germany

36

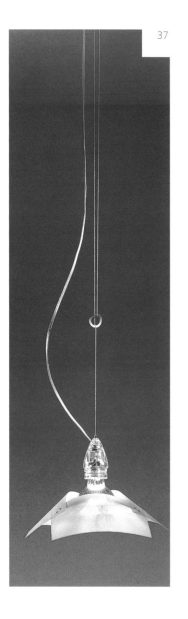

37

38

39

38

Maurizio
Ferrari

Table lamp
Astioca
Wood, Murano glass, chrome
3 x 60w bulbs
h 175cm di 41cm
h 68 ⅞ in di 16 ⅛ in
Manufacturer
Solzi Luce srl, Italy

39

Francesco
Lucchese

Standard lamp
Hermes
Silkscreened polycarbonate
250w halogen bulb and 100w incandescent bulb
h 180cm di of base 32cm
h 70 ⅞ in di of base 12 ⅝ in
Manufacturer
Luxo Italiana SpA, Italy

40

40

Marc **Newson**

Standard lamp
Helice
Aluminium, glass
300w linear halogen bulb
h 190cm di 36cm
h 74⅞in di 14⅛in
Manufacturer
Flos SpA, Italy

41

Woka

Suspension light
Noadela

Standard lamp
Fabodestra
Brass
3 x 100w, 3 x 40w bulbs
Noadela: h 200cm di 50cm
h 78⅜in di 19⅝in
Fabodestra: h 180cm di 50cm
h 70⅞in di 19⅝in
Manufacturer
Woka Lamps Vienna, Austria

41

Profile

Wolfgang Karolinsky

Wolfgang Karolinsky is one of the most influential figures in Austrian lighting design. Yet, by his own admission, he is not a designer. He is a lighting entrepreneur – or rather a lighting archaeologist – who has made his name rediscovering and reissuing modern lighting classics from the early years of this century. Among the forgotten or obscure design gems he has rescued are architectural lights by Hoffmann, Moser, Wagner and Loos, including Hoffmann's fittings for Villa Spitzer (1901–02) and Palais Stoclet (1905–11).

His small, Vienna-based company Woka Lamps – the name is an amalgam of his first name and surname – has built an international reputation for its faithful reproductions of Wiener Werkstätte classics, using original tools, techniques and patents. Every piece is handmade. The fitting shown here is typical of Karolinsky's approach. It is a French uplighter from the late 1920s with the unusual feature of three thin light sources radiating from its stem. Its designer is unknown. Karolinksy bought the original light in Vienna and was so charmed by its design that he decided to reproduce it.

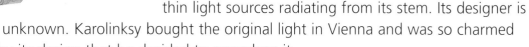

Karolinsky's obsession with Modern Movement lighting began when he was a music student at university in Vienna in the 1970s. To finance his studies, he worked in a flea-market selling Art Nouveau and Jugendstil lamps. Gradually the vacation job became a career, and Karolinsky has been playing a different tune ever since. Aside from his workshop, his Woka Gallery in a baroque seventeenth-century palace in the centre of Vienna is a focal point for turn-of-the-century lights.

Woka has attracted a firm following among architects and specifiers, especially in Germany which is the company's largest market. A fastidious approach to buying up copyrights to designs and original press tools from the Austrian companies who first made the light classics has resulted in products of rare quality and historical authenticity. But Karolinsky has an eye to the future as well as the past, and uses the allure of the classics to finance eclectic collections of new design. Among his current collaborators are Eichinger & Knechtl, protégés of the architect Hans Hollein, and Viennese architect Gabriele Sinzinger, who has designed a new family of adjustable ceiling lamps for Woka. Karolinsky suggests that his new designs might become 'the antiques of tomorrow', but admits that 'beautiful lamps are luxury items – people can live without them'.

41

Mezzo Restaurant
London, UK
Designer
Marlin

Light has always been central to the success of Sir Terence Conran's London restaurants. In Quaglino's in the West End, Conran worked with Marlin to create an ingenious illuminated skylight which runs the length of the basement eaterie. Now, at Mezzo, a far larger but equally glamorous 700-seater restaurant on the original site of the Marquee Club, he has collaborated with the same lighting design team. The result is a vibrant scheme which spectacularly overcomes the potential for gloom given the vast scale of the place.

The main lighting is unobtrusively provided by Marlin low-voltage tungsten halogen downlights, all on individual transformers. A sophisticated dimming system allows staff total flexibility in setting light levels, while the interior design emphasis on mirrored walls, pale surfaces, white table cloths and gleaming chrome helps to reflect light into every corner. 'I hope Mezzo gives people such a thrill that their jaws drop when they see it for the first time,' says Conran. A key part of the drama of Mezzo is the kitchen areas which are open to the view of diners. Here, the lighting is necessarily functional with a minimum lux level of 300, in contrast to the more decorative lighting approach in the restaurant, with average lux levels of 250. Fibre optics also play a role, downlighting one intimate, enclosed dining area, and enhancing the innovative design of an upstairs bar.

Above
General restaurant view showing the staircase leading down from the mezzanine eaterie to the main floor, with flexible light levels enhancing the mood.

Right
Mirrored walls reflect the low-voltage tungsten-halogen downlights.

LaSalle National Bank

Chicago, USA
Designer
Schuler & Shook

The main banking hall of the LaSalle National Bank in Chicago was originally built in 1928, complete with fine architectural detail, elegant chandeliers and an art glass skylight that filled the hall with daylight. In 1961, air-conditioning was installed in the hall, the skylight was roofed over, and the chandeliers were replaced by incandescent downlights. The hall has now been restored to its former glory in a sensitive scheme designed by architects VOA Associates and lighting consultants Schuler & Shook.

Schuler & Shook's work set out to add visual drama to the space while maintaining consistency of light on work surfaces. The project's key lighting elements do not slavishly recreate the past but reinterpret it in a fresh, contemporary way. Thus the decision was made to illuminate the art glass ceiling artificially using an array of 180 four-lamp fluorescent fixtures, suspended by chain 48 inches above the glass, rather than recreate the daylighting effect. A network of catwalks, also suspended from the skylight framework, was designed to service these fixtures, while a layer of white frosted laminated glass was inserted to diffuse reflections through the clear art glass. In addition, rather than reproduce the original chandeliers, new frosted acrylic bowls with polished brass trim were custom-designed by the renovation team to uplight the ceiling and supplement the general lighting.

Views of the newly refurbished main banking hall of the LaSalle National Bank in Chicago show the splendid art glass skylight restored in all its glory and lit by suspended fluorescents. Perimeter chandeliers are new designs, not reproductions, which uplight the ceiling.

Go Shoe Shop

Hamburg, Germany
Designer
Torsten Neeland

This jewel of a shoe shop in a turn-of-the-century Hamburg
building creates an entire architectural setting out of pure
planes of indirect light. Designer Torsten Neeland has turned the
35 square-metre retail space, organized over two floors, into a
smooth, neutral canvas and has painted it with light. As he
explains, 'Next to the lighting, only colour and space should
exist.'

The scheme, explains Neeland, has three main elements: ambient
light, to orient customers; focal glow, to draw attention to the
shoes, which are displayed as modern artworks; and a play of
blue brilliance, which gives the space depth. The ambient and
focal lighting is achieved by using Osram warm-white Tone 31
fluorescent lamps; the brilliant blue lighting, by using TLD Philips
fluorescent lamps. Guzzini entrance spots provide a hint of
what lies inside. Neeland handled the lighting concept and all
the design and technical details himself. He says he has been
fascinated by lighting since he began designing light fittings as a
student at Hamburg College of Art.

This indirect lighting scheme for a Hamburg shoe store in a turn-of-the-century building dissolves the material environment until only light, colour and space exist. The blue lighting suggests depth within the small store. Torsten Neeland paints with light on a smooth, neutral canvas, using indirect fluorescents to display shoes as contemporary artworks.

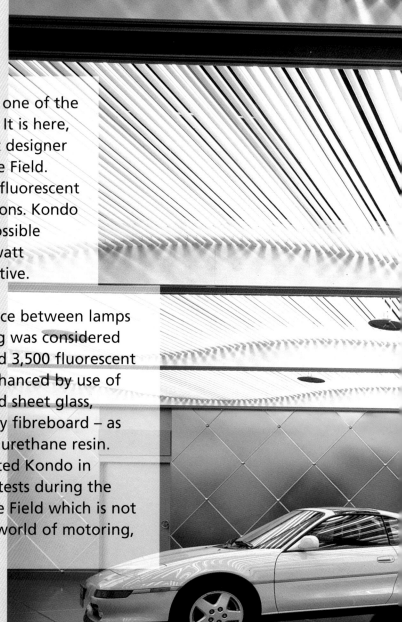

Toyota Car Showroom

Osaka, Japan
Designer
Yasuo Kondo

Amlux's 'Toyota town' in Osaka has been described as one of the
world's most sophisticated car retailing environments. It is here,
on the third floor at the very top of the building, that designer
Yasuo Kondo has created a large showroom called The Field.
This sits beneath an artificial sky comprising waves of fluorescent
lamp louvres across the ceiling to suggest cloud formations. Kondo
wanted to make the cars for sale look as natural as possible
under a uniform light, so he experimented with 110-watt
fluorescent lamps fixed to louvres to achieve his objective.

Tests on the span of the waves and the distance between lamps
and louvres were carried out until the lighting was considered
sufficiently flat, soft and human. In all, around 3,500 fluorescent
lamps were used. The lighting was further enhanced by use of
reflective wall surfaces – including sandblasted sheet glass,
aluminium panels, and coated medium-density fibreboard – as
well as a showroom floor coated in a smooth urethane resin.
Consultants Lighting Planners Associates assisted Kondo in
developing his ideas and carried out lighting tests during the
project. The result is a lighting scheme for The Field which is not
just original in concept; in the often frenetic world of motoring,
it achieves just the right calming effect.

Waves of fluorescent lamp louvres mimic cloud formations in a Toyota car showroom called The Field. The design aim was to create a flat, soft and uniform lighting ambience. Approximately 3,500 110-watt fluorescent lamps were used.

Left
    Lighting plays a significant
    role in creating levels of
    transparency throughout
    this advertising office, in
    combination with clear, etched
    and black transparent glass.

Right
    Tall glass light towers and blue
    rope lighting suspended from
    the black ceiling lend a sense
    of creativity and dynamism to
    the agency's video conference
    centre.

Ackerman McQueen
Advertising Offices

Tulsa, Oklahoma, USA
Designer
Hunzicker Brothers Lighting
Elliott & Associates Architects

The light, structure and volumes of this top-floor space in a 1917 Oklahoma office building (the original drawing room for the geological department of the Carter Oil Company) encouraged lighting designer Phil Easlon and architect Rand Elliott to create a stage-set environment representing 'the inside of an idea'. The office features a poured-in-place concrete structure with 14- and 18-foot high ceilings, skylight openings and clerestory windows. The design team used light in combination with clear, etched and black transparent glass as an imaginative design tool to consciously shape forms and surfaces, introducing levels of transparency in a 'dramatic studio for creative thought'. Even the company logo is projected as light on to a concrete X-brace.

This is a scheme full of innovative ideas. A sculptural light box displays randomly taped advertising campaign images in a waiting area. Along one perimeter wall, a series of once-covered portholes set 12 inches off the ground sends orbs of light through the space. The creative department is flooded with natural light from clerestory windows, while suspended fabric lights hang from steel trusses to illuminate the central spaces. The heart of the project is, however, a video-conferencing centre. Here, 18-foot-tall etched glass light towers glow in the dark, while blue rope lighting 'floats' down from the black ceiling. Even the wire-pull chain switches for lights in the conference rooms were fashioned by a local artist.

Hagia Sophia
Instanbul, Turkey
Designer
Erco Lighting in co-operation with
Total Aydinlatma Mümessillik (Istanbul)

Above left
Wall-mounted Trion uplighters
from Erco illuminate the Hagia
Sophia's mosaics.

Above
A view of the main interior
below the dome shows the
importance of daylighting to
this masterpiece of architectural
history. Eclipse spotlights
provide brilliant light accents
and ensure optimum colour
rendition.

Right
Precious gold mosaics in the
aisles are accentuated by
uplighters on Hi-trac light
structures.

Built in 532 AD as a symbol of the power and grandeur of the Byzantine Empire of Justinian I, the Hagia Sophia is one of the great masterpieces of architectural history and one of the most enduring expressions of daylight as an essential element of architecture. The centrepiece of this domed basilica is the extraordinary dome itself, 56 metres high and measuring 33 metres in diameter. According to the Greek historian Procopius, it appears 'as if suspended from heaven on golden chains'. Late Byzantine mosaics and an unusually large collection of historical and religious relics make this holy place an environment of shimmering spirituality requiring the utmost care in restoration.

Erco's artificial lighting scheme is dedicated to providing discreet and carefully targeted support in order to accentuate the church's unique intensity and beauty. Where wall-mounting was possible, mosaics are lit by Trion uplighters. In other areas, low-voltage halogen Eclipse spotlights – set on tracks or at the side of window sills – accent masterpieces of devotional art. The result is a scheme that firmly directs the visitor's eye while remaining true to the abstract religiosity of the original. The architectural renovation was under the direction of a scientific committee of professors and architects.

The Royal Pavilion
Brighton, UK
Designer
John Bradley Associates

A scheme to floodlight the Brighton Pavilion as the culmination of a four-year restoration programme has shed new light on one of Britain's strangest and most fascinating historical monuments. The building that George IV created as a winter residence in the style of a romantic Oriental Regency palace demanded sensitive illumination of its façades to reveal the rich architectural detail unapparent during daylight hours. The designer, John Bradley Associates, also faced other challenges, not least the need to achieve sympathetic colour rendering of the stonework in choice of light source, and exercise care in fixing cables and fittings in the fabric of a Grade 1 listed building.

The result is a complex and masterful scheme which sculpts the building with light, avoiding the flattening effects of lighting upwards or at right angles to surfaces. Light and shade are created on the myriad of shapes, hollows and projections that form the essential character of the Pavilion. Fourteen different types of fitting, varying in size, wattage and beam distribution, have been used – 200 spotlights and floodlights in all, their position carefully plotted at the design stage during careful analysis of the Pavilion's structure. High-pressure sodium discharge lamps were chosen as the light source, for their long-life efficiency and colour rendering, while special fixing brackets avoided damage to the structural envelope.

Rear view of the Royal Pavilion, Brighton. The lighting of the façades reveals a wealth of architectural detail unapparent during daylight hours. High-pressure sodium achieves sensitive colour rendering in a scheme which uses 200 spotlights and floodlights to sculpt the building with light. All the lamps and fittings were supplied by Philips.

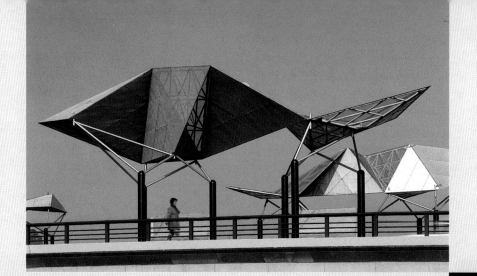

Shirakawa Bridge

Kumamoto, Japan
Designer
Kazuko Fujie

Shirakawa Bridge, the central bridge in the city of Kumamoto in southern Japan, has been given a spectacular new personality with the introduction of a series of *Flying Lights* designed by Kazuko Fujie. The bridge is 150 metres long and carries a major city road. In a total refurbishment programme, it has been given new road widths, guard rails, sidewalks and pavement patterns. But the most dramatic aspect of the project is the ethereal and floating lighting designs which change the experience of crossing the river. As Fujie explains: 'The ambiguous and shifting form of the lights gives expression to people's memories and impressions of the city.'

The lights, which use an HID lamp source, are formed by clusters of coloured expanded steel with many intersecting angles. Light filters through the irregular planes and, due to their varying shape and orientation, a kaleidoscopic effect is produced. Since the project has been completed, the number of pedestrians and car users crossing this old bridge has increased, reflecting its status as a source of pride for the people of the city and as a tourist attraction. The bridge has even been chosen by television producers as the region's identity for a weather programme.
(See profile of Kazuko Fujie, page 27.)

Kazuko Fujie's *Flying Lights* span a major city bridge with clusters of expanded steel. Each surface is a different irregular triangle. During the day the lights form canopies to give protection from the elements; at night they take on a new luminous character.

The prominent location of this glazed office building designed by Nicholas Grimshaw & Partners at a busy international airport imposed severe constraints on its external lighting. The British Airways Compass Centre at Heathrow needed to stand out from surrounding buildings but not interfere with the vision of incoming pilots. To reduce the inevitable reflections that would result from lighting the glazed cladding from a distance, and because site restrictions did not allow use of fixtures off-building, consultant Equation Lighting Design located lighting equipment close to the structure.

There are three elements to the project. First, a custom-designed kerbstone detail – fluorescent tubes in a special asymmetric housing – at the base of the building provides a bed of light on which the Compass Centre appears to sit. Second, a *bris-soleil* at roof level houses pairs of compact fluorescent washlights which visually echo the architectural grid of the building. Third, metal-halide projectors mounted on cantilever brackets illuminate the curved aluminium corner cladding. All fittings were either manufactured or supplied by Concord Lighting. The combination of uplight from the base and washlight from the top of the building ensures that the entire façade is skilfully lit in a way that does not provide Air Traffic Control with a problem.

The jury of the International Association of Lighting Designers, in giving this scheme a top award in 1995, commented: 'The lighting design is the architecture.'

British Airways Compass Centre

Heathrow Airport, UK

Designer

Equation Lighting Design

Left and right
Fluorescent tubes in a special asymmetric 'Kerbstone' housing give the impression that the Compass Centre is resting on a bed of light, while compact fluorescent washlights at roof level reflect the architectural rhythm of the building.

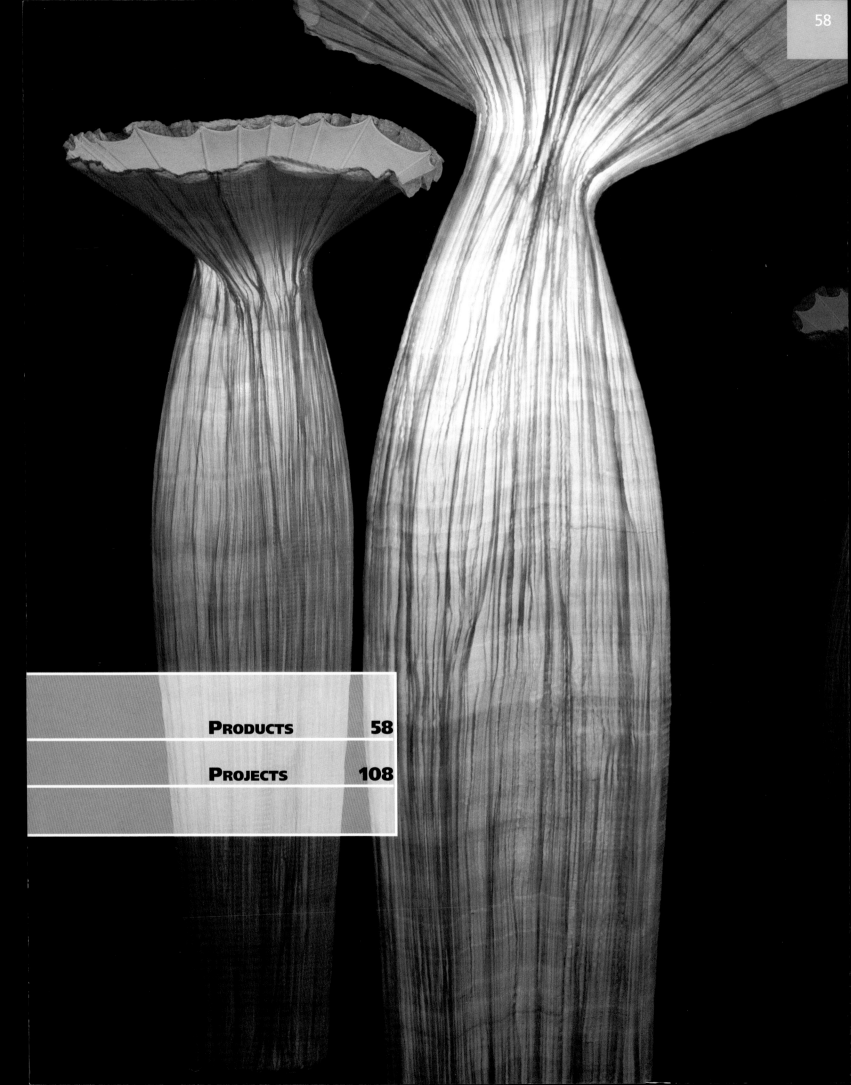

Art of the Decorative

Poul Henningsen, the Danish designer who created some of this century's most elegant lighting classics, once wrote: 'A thing is not beautiful until it is correctly formed and it is not right until it is beautifully formed.' This section looks at products and projects that possess the decorative appeal of fantasy and imagination, by combining utility and beauty. It celebrates the unusual, the offbeat and the inspirational in lighting design. Included among the table lamps, chandeliers and light sculptures shown here are specials, one-offs and prototypes.

Each piece expresses

a decorative artistic intent while remaining a functional tool to diffuse and direct light. The designers profiled each communicate a creative prowess in a range of different media – from the delicate ceramic lights of Japan's Masatoshi Sakaegi to the organic silk sculptures of Israel's Ayala Sperling-Serfaty, and the medieval arrow lights of French fashion designer Jean-Charles de Castelbajac.

The selection of projects, too, demonstrates the art of the decorative – from a Chilean telecommunications tower bathed in light of changing colours to the Gulf Coast casino lit in a sensual way that does not resort to neon kitsch.

2

1
(pages 58-9)

Ayala Sperling-
Serfaty

See page 80

2

Russell
Barker

Pendant
Sirius Mushroom
Glass, reinforced plastic
Max. 100w bulb
l 30cm di 24cm
l 11¾in di 9½in
Limited batch production
Manufacturer
SKK Lighting, UK

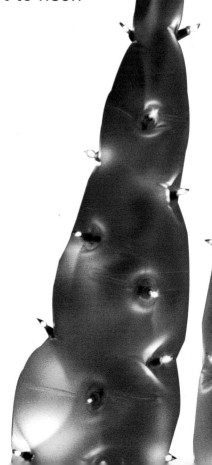

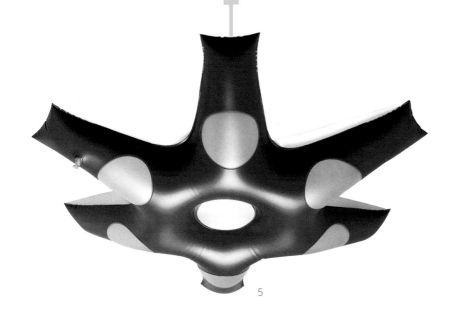

5

5

Nicholas
Crosbie

Suspension light
Blow
PVC
Fluorescent bulbs
h 15cm di 80cm
h 5 ⅞in di 31 ½in
Manufacturer
Inflate, UK

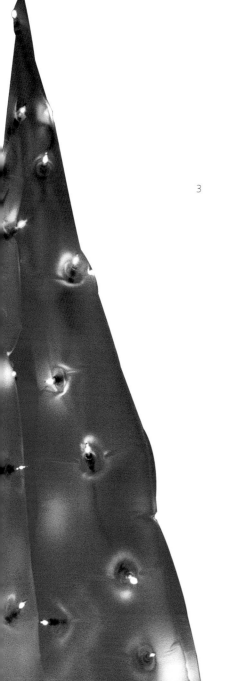

3

3

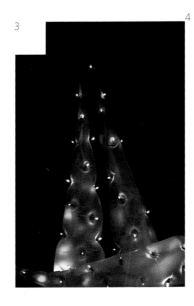

4

3

Katrien
Van Liefferinge

Luminosa series
No. 3
PVC
Fairy lights
h 100cm   di 20cm
h 39⅜in di 7⅞in
Limited batch production

4

Katrien
Van Liefferinge

Luminosa series
No. 2
Soft PVC, MDF
Compact fluorescent bulb
h 120–220cm di 32–56cm
h 47¼–86⅝in di 12⅝–22in
Limited batch production

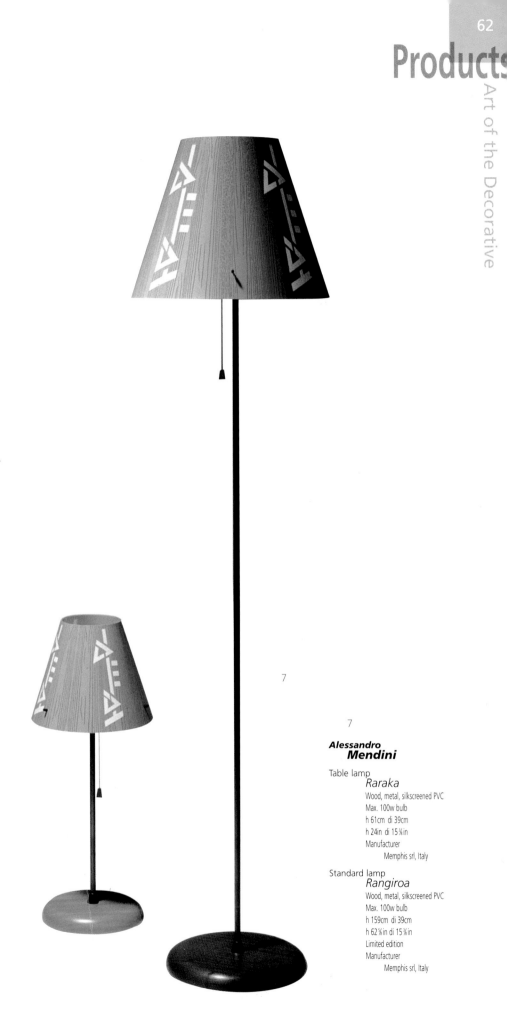

6

6

Masafumi
Katsukawa

Standard lamp
Papa Luce/Mamma Luce
Copper-plated metal
50w 12v halogen bulb
h 110cm w 40cm d 16cm
h 43⅜in w 15¾in d 6½in
Prototype

7

7

Alessandro
Mendini

Table lamp
Raraka
Wood, metal, silkscreened PVC
Max. 100w bulb
h 61cm di 39cm
h 24in di 15⅜in
Manufacturer
Memphis srl, Italy

Standard lamp
Rangiroa
Wood, metal, silkscreened PVC
Max. 100w bulb
h 159cm di 39cm
h 62⅝in di 15⅜in
Limited edition
Manufacturer
Memphis srl, Italy

8

Sarah
Reilly

Light/table
Table en Chemise
Steel, bronze, copper, silver, glass
Halogen bulb
h 75cm di 50cm
h 29½ in di 19⅝ in
Limited batch production

9

Sarah
Reilly

Sculptural light
Meteorlite
Steel, bronze, copper, silver, glass
Daylight bulb
h 85cm   w 35cm d 25cm
h 33½ in w 13¾ in d 9⅞ in
Limited batch production

8

9

11

10

10

Masafumi
Katsukawa

Table lamp and ceiling light
Sub
Chromed metal
50w 12v dichroic bulb
h 46cm di 12cm
h 18⅛in di 4¾in
Limited batch production
Manufacturer
Lumen Centre Italia srl, Italy

11

Johanna
Grawunder

Wall light
No. 60
Polished stainless steel
Neon bulb
h 44cm w 23cm d 15cm
h 17⅜in w 9in d 5⅞in
Limited batch of six
Manufacturer
The Gallery Mourmans, The Netherlands

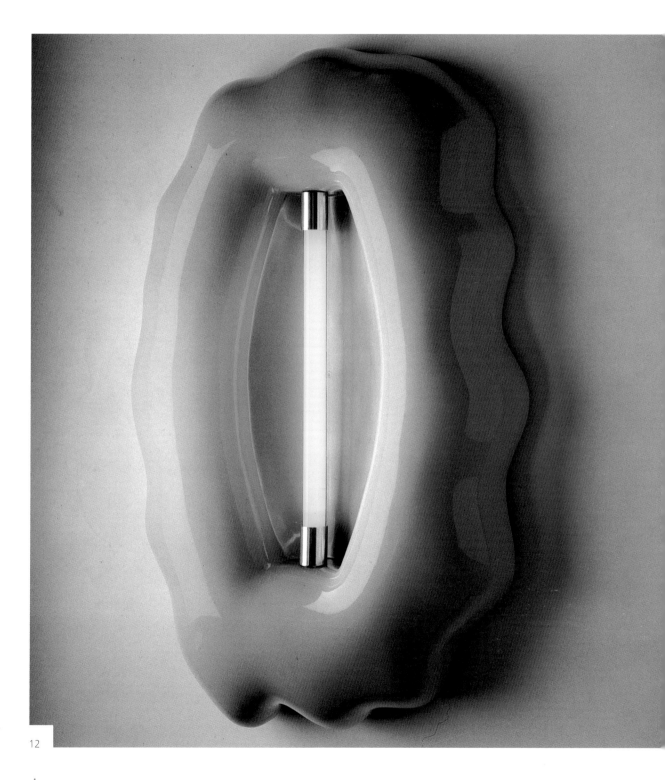

12

Ettore
Sottsass

Wall light
No. 27
Gellcoat fibreglass
Neon bulb
h 82cm w 42cm d 6cm
h 32 ¼ in w 16 ½ in d 2 ¼ in
Limited batch of six
Manufacturer
The Gallery Mourmans, The Netherlands

13

Ingo Maurer

Chandelier
Porca Miseria
Metal, porcelain
600–700w bulb
h 150cm di 110cm
h 59in di 43¼in
Limited batch production
Manufacturer
Ingo Maurer GmbH, Germany

14

Ingo Maurer

Wall light
One for the Recession
Lacquered steel
60w 230v halogen bulb
w 21cm l 41cm
w 8¼in l 16⅛in
Limited batch production
Manufacturer
Ingo Maurer GmbH, Germany

Ingo *Maurer*

Ingo Maurer has been the most consistently original talent on the European lighting scene for the past 30 years. Since he first achieved prominence with his giant *Bulb Clear* lamp in 1966, based on the Pop Art of Jasper Johns, this German designer who trained originally as a typographer, has constantly surprised and delighted his audience with a succession of poetic, imaginative and often whimsical innovations in light. 'I'm still searching for different ways to create lights,' he asserts. 'To rest on your laurels and just do a lot of business with existing products would be too boring for words.'

Maurer's great gift is to marry the technical and the aesthetic in a surprisingly holistic way. As Vico Magistretti remarked of his work: 'Ingo uses technology as a means of expressing a new sense of beauty.' His Munich-based company, Ingo Maurer, designs, makes and sells lights without the aid of a retail showroom. Around 60 per cent of Maurer's work is centred on one-off, large-scale project installations: he has, for example, recently produced stunning designs for Ron Arad's foyer areas in the new Tel Aviv Opera House and for the Louisiana Museum in Copenhagen. The other 40 per cent comprises catalogue collections of wall and hanging lights, systems, table and standard lamps. 'When I started, I was interested in forms but now I'm more interested in the quality of light itself,' he explains. 'It gives me such a good feeling.'

Among his recent designs, the *Porca Miseria* fitting in white porcelain (opposite) was originally designed for a client with 'a slick, glossy, perfect kitchen – I wanted to break up the slickness of that kitchen! I always liked the idea of the explosion in slow motion, as seen in the film *Zabriski Point*.' His *Los Minimalos* task light, however, has a different purpose (see page 128). 'I've always been attracted by minimalism,' says Maurer. 'The relationship between the effort and the result is so important. It shouldn't take a lot of effort to produce a good result.'

Too much lighting today, he suggests, strains for effect and is ultimately self-defeating. That is the ultimate crime for a designer who trusts his emotions and has a running joke in his lights on the theme of the kitsch red throbbing heart. His latest version is entitled *One for the Recession*. 'I like to be playful,' says Maurer, 'and people need to be playful with light.'

15

16

David
D'Imperio

Standard lamp
Virosa

Brass, maple wood, polycarbonate
35w 12v halogen bulb
h 152cm w 15cm d 30.5cm
h 60in w 6in d 12in
Limited batch production
Manufacturer
David D'Imperio, USA

David
D'Imperio

Desk light
Virosa

Brass, steel, wood
20w 12v halogen bulb
h 25–86cm w 15cm d 15cm
h 10–34in w 6in d 6in
Limited batch production
Manufacturer
David D'Imperio, USA

David
D'Imperio

Suspension light
Lasio

Wood, brass, aluminium, plastic
50w 12v halogen bulb
h 152cm w 15cm l 15cm
h 60in w 6in l 6in
Limited batch production
Manufacturer
David D'Imperio, USA

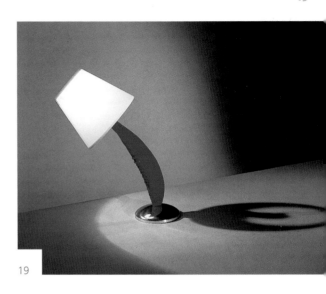

18

19

18

Harry Villiers

Standard lamp
Gauze
Stainless steel gauze, mild cast zinc
240v bulb
h 178cm di of base 17cm
h 70in di of base 6⅝in
Limited batch production
Manufacturer
Villiers Brothers, UK

19

Tim Villiers

Table lamp
Chilli
Silk velvet, cast aluminium, flexi-tube
60w 240v bulb
h 47cm di of base 12.5cm
h 18½in di of base 4⅞in
Limited batch production
Manufacturer
Villiers Brothers, UK

Harry and Tim
Villiers

Standard lamp
Benson
Silk velvet, flexi-tube, foam
240v bulb
h 115cm di of base 30cm
h 45¼in di of base 11⅞in
Limited batch production
Manufacturer
        Villiers Brothers, UK

21

22

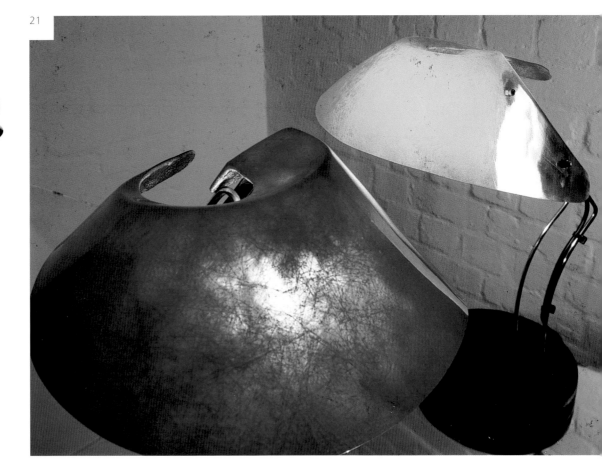

21

Ashley
Hall

Desk light
Teller
GRP, polyurethane, chrome steel
40w 240v tungsten bulb
h 38cm w 23cm l 32cm
h 15in w 9in l 12⅝in
Manufacturer
SKK Lighting, UK

22

Mark
McDonnell

Table lamp
Blown glass, wood
Incandescent bulb
h 46cm w 15cm
h 18in w 6in
Prototype

23

24

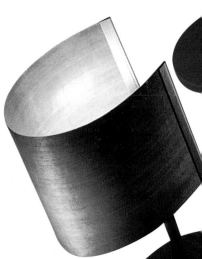

23

Anna
Gili

Table lamp
Cat
Opaflex (glass–plastic material)
100w bulb
h 87cm w 57cm d 15cm
h 34 ¼ in w 22 ⅛ in d 5 ⅞ in
Manufacturer
    SLAMP (trademark of Samuel Parker srl), Italy

24

Ernesto
Gismondi

and Giancarlo
Fassina

Table lamp/night light
Arcadia
Chromed metal, wood, glass
1 x 100w bulb (table), 1 x 60w bulb (night)
Table lamp: h 46cm di 36cm
h 18 ⅛ in di 14 ⅛ in
Night light: h 33.5cm di 26cm
h 13 ⅛ in di 10 ¼ in
Manufacturer
    Artemide SpA, Italy

26

25

25

Paolo
Golinelli

Table lamp
Ella
Wood, metal
Max. 40w frosted E14 bulb
h 45cm di 22cm
h 17 ¾ in di 8 ¾ in
Manufacturer
Ravarini Castoldi & Co., Italy

26

Maria Christina
Hamel

Table lamp
Zaza
Ceramic
60w bulb
h 52cm di 27cm
h 20 ½ in di 10 ⅝ in
Manufacturer
Marioni Paolo srl, Italy

28

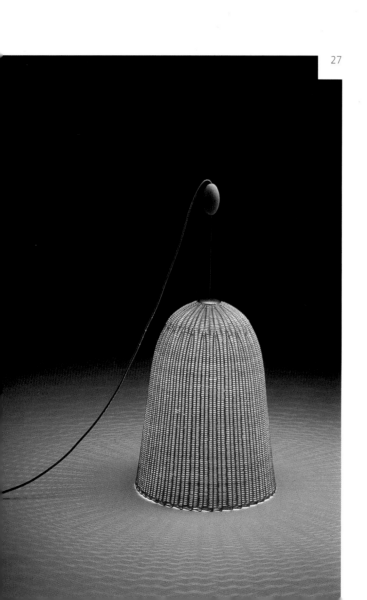

27

27

Paolo
Golinelli

Standard lamp
Aurora
Rattan core, metal, wood
Max. 100w bulb
h 115cm   di 50cm
h 45¼in di 19⅝in
Limited batch production
Manufacturer
Vittorio Bonacina & Co., Italy

28

Zeukyau
Shichida

Series of lights
Eboshi
Bamboo, paper, steel
Standard bulb
h 30–95cm di 16–40cm
h 11¾–37⅜in di 6½–15¾in
Limited batch production
Manufacturer
Kwau Shau An, Japan

29

29

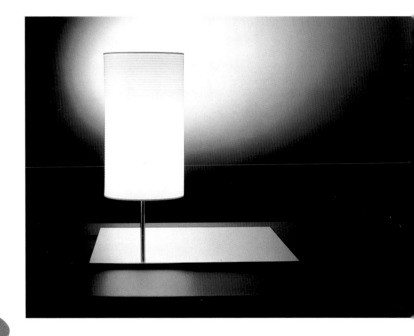

29   29

Josep
Aregall

Series of lights
Hold Me Tender

Metal, opaline corrugated polycarbonate
3 x 60w bulb (standard), 2 x 100w bulb
(suspension), max. 60w bulb (table)
Standard lamp, *Hong Kong:*
h 111cm di 41cm
h 43⅜in di 16⅛in
Standard lamp, *Kowloon:*
h 45cm di 61cm
h 17¾in di 24in
Suspension light, *Alvar:*
h 20cm di 65cm
h 7⅞in di 25⅝in
Table lamp, *Double Bay:*
h 41cm di 40cm
h 16⅛in di 15¾in
Manufacturer
        Metalarte SA, Spain

30

Ayala Sperling-
Serfaty

Wall light
Miduza

Metal, silk

di 35cm

di 13¾in

Limited batch production

Manufacturer

        Aqua Creations, Israel

31

Ayala Sperling-
Serfaty

Wall light
Shellight 2

Metal, silk

h 80cm w 35cm

h 31½in w 13¾in

Limited batch production

Manufacturer

        Aqua Creations, Israel

32

Ayala Sperling-
Serfaty

Table lamp
Palms

Silk, organza, metal

3 x 100w bulbs

h 80cm di 80cm

h 31½in di 31½in

Limited batch production

Manufacturer

        Aqua Creations, Israel

30

32

31

Ayala Sperling-
Serfaty

Standard lamp
Mermaid
Metal, silk
h 130cm di 45cm
h 51 ⅛in di 17 ¾in
Limited batch production
Manufacturer
        Aqua Creations, Israel

Ayala Sperling-
Serfaty

Wall light
Fan
Silk, metal, lead
60w bulb
w 40cm l 27cm d 22cm
w 15 ¾in l 10 ¾in d 8 ⅝in
Limited batch production
Manufacturer
        Aqua Creations, Israel

34

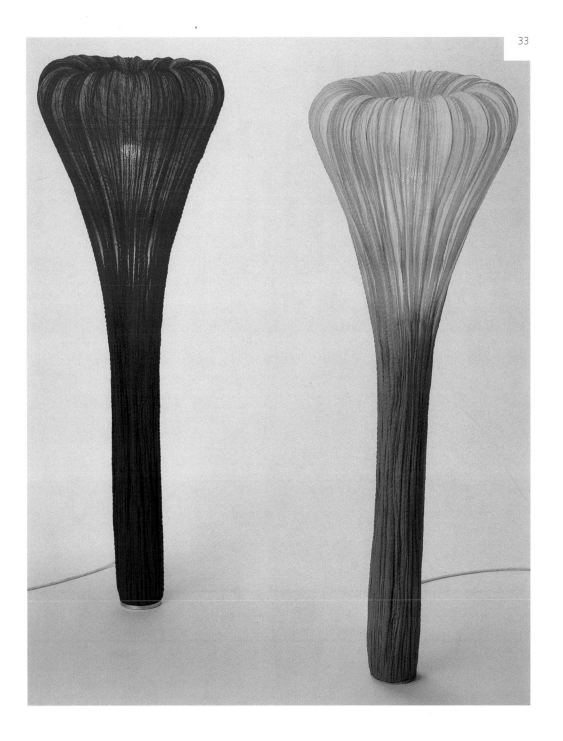

33

35

35

**Ayala Sperling-
Serfaty**

Standard lamp
Morning Glory
Metal, silk
2 x 100v bulbs
h 190–230cm di 80–100cm
h 74¼–90½in di 31½–39⅜in
Limited batch production
Manufacturer
    Aqua Creations, Israel

36

36

**Ayala Sperling-
Serfaty**

Wall/ceiling light
Spider Coral
Metal, silk
3 x 60v bulbs
w 80cm l 130cm d 22cm
w 31½in l 51⅛in d 8⅝in
Limited batch production
Manufacturer
    Aqua Creations, Israel

Ayala *Sperling-Serfaty*

Israeli lighting and furniture designer Ayala Sperling-Serfaty trained as a fine artist and it is this sensibility that informs so much of her highly original work. After military service and art college in Tel Aviv and Jerusalem, she studied for three years at Middlesex Polytechnic in the UK during the 1980s, working mainly on sculpture. Today, her organic pieces, whether seating made of fruit or ceiling lights resembling exotic flowers, possess a sculptural quality. Lighting especially fascinates her. As she explains, 'Lighting is something very beautiful. You take a sculpture with see-through materials and place a light source inside and then you can do wonderful things.'

Today, Ayala Sperling-Serfaty works from her own studio, Aqua Creations, in Tel Aviv, producing beautiful batch-made products. Her *Spider Coral* light in metal and silk started life as a project for a hotel. The intention was to create an entire ceiling comprising several of the objects. But the architect lost the project so Sperling-Serfaty adapted the design for domestic use. *Morning Glory*, another popular design, is a free-standing lamp up to 2.3 metres in height, produced in such a way that each one is slightly different. Groups of five have been specified for hotels and even offices, indicating a growing interest by users in having more natural, sensual light objects around them.

Sperling-Serfaty says that the sculptress and fine artist Eva Hesse is a major influence on her work: 'Eva Hesse was part of the New York scene in the 1950s and 60s, and she did marvellous things with see-through materials. Many of my designs relate to her work.' Another inspiration are the crushed silk dresses of Japanese fashion designer Issey Miyake.

One can see Ayala Sperling-Serfaty, aged 34, as belonging to an exciting new generation of Israeli designers, led by Ron Arad and Yaacov Kaufman, who today command international attention. 'There isn't really a culture of visual things here, but more designers are working and doing well in Israel,' Sperling-Serfaty confirms. What is the reason? 'All the cities are so new, apart from Jerusalem,' she speculates. 'The architecture is quite poor with second-rate materials, because everything has been built so quickly with no cash. But because everything is so ugly, people have an open mind about design. Really, designers and artists in Israel have a lot to do.'

35

37

Masayo
Ave

Standard lamp
Mymble
Wood, Shibori textile
60w bulb
h 110cm di 33cm
h 43 ¼in di 13in
Limited batch production
Manufacturer
        Ave Design Corporation, Japan

38

Leonid
Yentus

Table lamp
Moonrise in Jersey City
Aluminium, adhesive films, magnetic plastic
2 x 100w halogen bulbs
h 80cm w 30cm l 30cm
h 31 ½ in w 11 ⅞ in l 11 ⅞ in
Prototype
Manufacturer
    Y Design, USA

39

39

Louis
Lara

Table lamp
Silo
Aluminium, parafin-coated paper
Compact fluorescent or 60w incandescent bulb
h 48cm di 13cm
h 18 ¾in di 5in
Manufacturer
Dansk Lights Inc., USA

40

40

Louis
Lara

Table lamp
Ela
Maple, steel, parafin-coated paper
Max. 40w candelabra bulb
h 38cm di 9cm
h 15in di 3 ½ in
Manufacturer
Dansk Lights Inc., USA

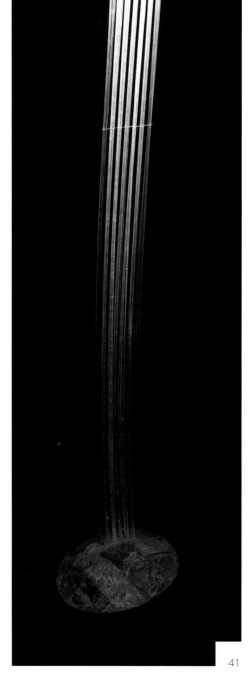

41

Leonid
Yentus

Standard lamp
Rain
Copper, brass, aluminium, acrylic
300w halogen bulb
h 190cm di 41 cm
h 74¾ in di 16¼ in
One-off
Manufacturer
        Y Design, USA

41

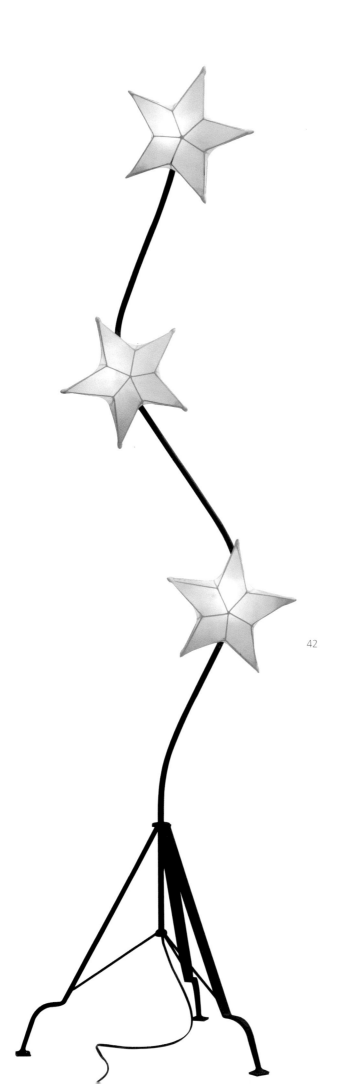

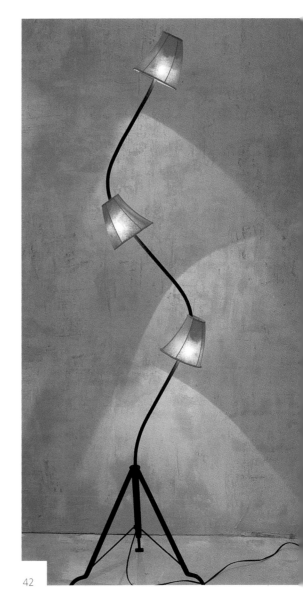

42

42

42

Paolo
Giordano

Standard lamp
Serpentine
Wrought iron, stretch fabric
3 x halogen bulbs
h 180cm w 45cm l 45cm
h 70⅞in w 17¾in l 17¾in
Manufacturer
    Zoltan, Italy

43

43

Paolo Bistacchi

and Lorenzo Stano

Suspension light
Luna
Aluminium, glass
2 x low-voltage standard bulbs
h max. 215cm   w 67cm
h max. 84⅝in   w 26⅜in
Manufacturer
Tre ci Luce, Italy

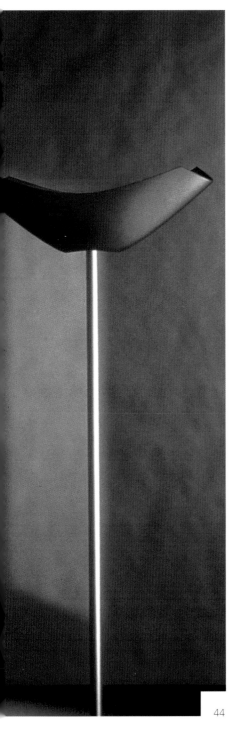

44

44

Josep
Lluscà

Series of lights
Servul
Metal, wood
300w linear halogen bulb
Standard lamp: h 190cm w 29cm
h 74 ⅞in w 11 ⅜in
Wall light: h 18cm w 29cm d 17cm
h 7in w 11 ⅜in   d 6 ¾in
Manufacturer
        Flos SpA, Italy

45

Marc
Harrison

Wall light/table lamp
Aphid Illuminant
Plywood, fabric, polycarbonate
Compact fluorescent incandescent bulb
h 30cm w 11cm l 30cm
h 11 ⅞in w 4 ⅜in l 11 ⅞in
Manufacturer
        ANTworks, Australia

44

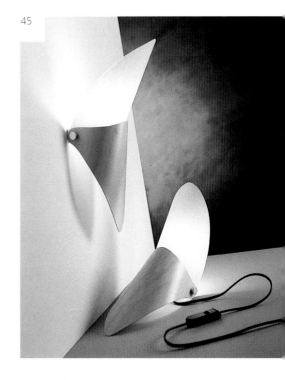

45

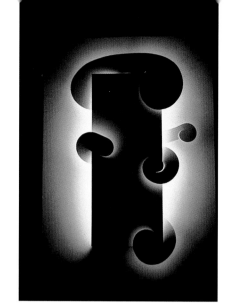

46

47

46

Masatoshi
Sakaegi

Wall light
Lighting Graphic A-E
Metal, paper
Fluorescent tube
h 115/90cm w 90/85/43cm d 16/14/12cm
h 45¼/35⅜in w 35⅜/33½/17in d 6⅓/5½/4⅜in
One-off
Manufacturer
Sakaegi Design Studio, Japan

47

Masatoshi
Sakaegi

Series of lights
Surface Tension
Bone china
40–60w mini-ball bulbs
h 19cm w 20cm l 20cm
h 7½in w 7⅞in l 7⅞in
Limited batch production
Manufacturer
Sakaegi Design Studio, Japan

Masatoshi *Sakaegi*

Japanese designer Masatoshi Sakaegi is an unusual talent on the lighting scene in that he insists he is first and foremost a designer of ceramics. His studio specializes in ceramic tableware, wall tiles and sculpture and he has received international attention for such sophisticated innovations as his textured, undulating *Waving Motion* and *Tension* relief wall tiles, which are inspired by Finnish design. Sakaegi works and teaches in Aichi Prefecture, which is responsible for almost two-thirds of Japan's ceramics production. Understandably, therefore, his foray into lighting has been largely based on the light-diffusing qualities of bone china.

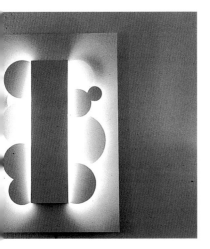

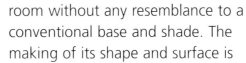

Usually, ceramics are only used for the base of a light fitting. But Masatoshi Sakaegi uses ceramics for the whole lamp, demonstrating his original approach to the material. Bone china has occasionally been used for delicate tableware and Sakaegi has developed this semi-transparency for use in lighting. His *Surface Tension* series presents a range of ceramic lightworks, each a piece of art radiating light to create a soft hue in a room without any resemblance to a conventional base and shade. The making of its shape and surface is unique. Special fabric is stretched over a number of wooden uprights placed on a board to produce the required texture and flowing three-dimensional shapes.

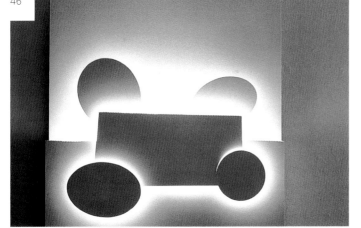

The *Surface Tension* series recently won a silver award for Sakaegi at the 4th International Ceramics Competition in Japan. One of the judges, Toshiyuki Kita, the leading furniture designer, was so impressed by the range's experimental creative process that he exclaimed: 'It's great! This ceramics designer has developed quite extraordinary lighting which lighting designers *per se* are unable to emulate.' Sakaegi himself observes: 'Ceramics can easily be adapted to any form and provide creative freedom. Moulds are cheap and flexible without requiring expensive tooling or the resources of a large factory.'

A principal attraction of ceramic material is that it can gently diffuse light, unlike metal, and resist heat without suitable air flow, unlike paper or fabric. But the resourceful Sakaegi has not confined himself to bone china in producing lighting. His *Graphic* wall lights use metal, paper and fluorescent lamps to play with patterns of light, shadow and form in a very appealing way. This work reflects the uninhibited artistic approach of a designer always alert to new material possibilities.

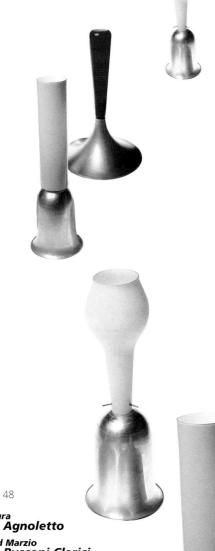

49

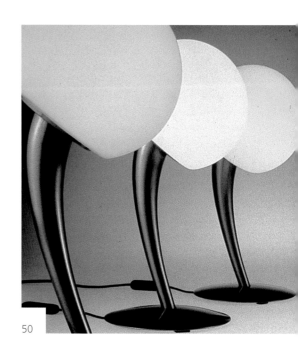

50

48

Laura
Agnoletto

and Marzio
Rusconi Clerici

Standard lamp
Totem 4
Aluminium, glass
60w bulb
h 50–60cm   di 50cm
h 19⅝–23⅝in   di 19⅝in
Manufacturer
Amedei Tre snc, Italy

49

Laura
Agnoletto

and Marzio
Rusconi Clerici

Table lamp
Mina N5
Perspex
Opaline incandescent bulb
h 30cm   di 20cm
h 11¾in   di 7⅞in
Manufacturer
Amedei Tre snc, Italy

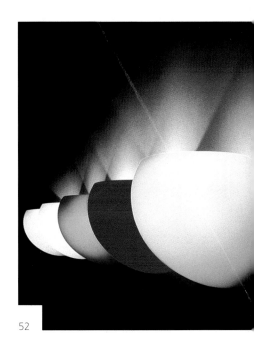

52

50

Roberto
Pamio

Table lamp
Inchino
Satin-finished blown glass
100w 220v bulb
h 43cm di 21cm
h 16⅞in di 8¼in
Manufacturer
New Leucos SpA, Italy

51

Oriano
Favaretto

Standard lamp
Poli Pò/R1
Satin-finished glass, wood, chrome
6 x 60w bulbs
h 152cm di 55cm
h 59⅞in di 21⅝in
Manufacturer
Vetreria de Majo srl, Italy

52

Renato
Toso

and Noti
Massari

Wall light
Golf P1
Murano glass
60w incandescent bulb, 150w halogen bulb
h 50cm di 42cm
h 19⅝in di 16½in
Manufacturer
Leucos srl, Italy

53

54

55

53

Arne
Jacobsen

and Enri
Moller

Suspension light
Aarhus
Brass or chrome plate, opaline glass
100w 220v bulb
h 15cm di 47cm
h 5⅞in di 18½in
Manufacturer
Santa & Cole Ediciones de Diseño SA, Spain

54

Sigeaki
Asahara

Suspension light
Olla
Satin-etched blown glass
Max. 100w bulb
h max. 175cm di 24cm
h max. 68⅛in di 9½in
Manufacturer
Lucitalia SpA, Italy

55

Tobias
Grau

Suspension light
Darling
Stainless steel, glass
150w halogen bulb
di 58cm
di 22⅞in
Manufacturer
Tobias Grau KG GmbH & Co., Germany

56   55   57

56

Arne
Jacobsen

and Enri
Moller

Suspension light
Aarhus
Brass or chrome plate, opaline glass
60w 220v bulb
h 25cm di 17.5cm
h 9¾in di 6¾in
Manufacturer
     Santa & Cole Ediciones de Diseño SA, Spain

57

Jordi Vilardell
Iglesias

Suspension light
Sinera
Iron, brass, inox, opaque glass
Max. 20w bulb
h 5cm l 64cm
h 2in l 25in
Manufacturer
     Gargot Disseny Meditterani SA, Spain

59

60

58

58

Sigeaki
Asahara

Wall light
Olla
Satin-etched blown glass
Max. 250w bulb
h 36cm d 31cm
h 14⅛in d 12⅛in
Manufacturer
Lucitalia SpA, Italy

59

Sigeaki
Asahara

Ceiling light
Olla
Satin-etched blown glass
Max. 100w bulb
h 35.5cm di 24cm
h 14in di 9½in
Manufacturer
Lucitalia SpA, Italy

60

Hans von
Klier

Standard lamp,
Piovra
Wood, steel, glass
240v halogen bulb
h 180cm di 40cm
h 71⅛in di 15¾in
Manufacturer
A. Bianchi srl, Italy

61   62   63

61

Sigeaki
Asahara

Table lamp
Olla
Satin-etched blown glass
Max. 250w bulb
h 42cm w 25cm
h 16 ½ in w 9 ¾ in
Manufacturer
Lucitalia SpA, Italy

62

Karim
Rashid

Standard lamp
Chora
Aluminium, lathed wood, blown glass, brass
100w incandescent bulb
h 100cm di 25cm
h 39 ¼ in di 9 ¾ in
One-off

63

Karim
Rashid

Table lamp
Orb
Blown glass, cherrywood
100w halogen quartz bulb
h 70cm w 25cm d 18cm
h 27 ½ in w 9 ¾ in d 7in
Prototype

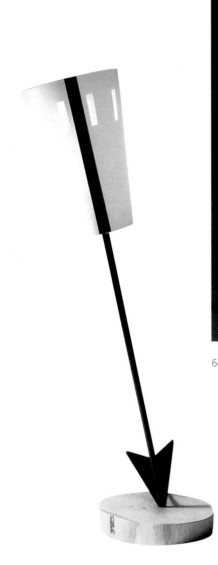

64

64

**Jean-Charles
de Castelbajac**

Desk light and standard lamp
Robin Wood
Wood, metal, polypropylene
60w bulb
Standard lamp:
h 180cm di 20cm
h 70⅛in di 7⅞in
Desk light:
h 60cm
h 23⅝in
Manufacturer
    Brossier Saderne, France

Jean-Charles de Castelbajac

French fashion designer Jean-Charles de Castelbajac brings a unique sensibility to the field of lighting. The man who cut a coat from his boarding school blanket to create his first fashion show, dressed Rod Stewart, mixed with Vivienne Westwood and Malcolm McLaren, designed the clothes for Woody Allen's film *Annie Hall*, and provided sweaters for Françoise Mitterrand, says he always needs to work with materials or concepts that have a 'natural eloquence'.

Light, he explains, 'has this natural eloquence more than anything else.' What matters to de Castelbajac is colour and form, especially colour which he describes as 'a means of proclaiming my convictions. If I've always loved primary colours in particular, it's because they represent life, energy and nature.' And light is a primary source of colour. Despite his prominent position in the fashion vanguard, de Castelbajac has always been attracted by adjacent design fields. In the early 1970s he joined Didier Grumbach and Andrée Putman's Créateurs et Industriels group. In the early 1980s, after meeting Raymond Loewy and Ettore Sottsass, he began designing furniture and lighting. His design of the *Proust Table* included a panel covered with the names of famous personalities. One of his first lights was made of porcelain, but his latest lighting pieces use wood, metal, plastics and glass.

What is so interesting about them is the way they distil his broader artistic preoccupations into a functional lighting tool. His *Robin Wood* lights, for example, reflect his self-image as 'a kind of hunter from the Middle Ages'. Bows and arrows crop up constantly in his quirky drawings and it is no surprise that they should form the basis for a range of lights. Equally, his *Seven Symbols* series of lights – *Moon*, *Sun*, *Heart*, *Crown*, *Star*, *Storm* and *Wing* – reflects his long-time interest in composing a very personal alphabet based on various well understood symbols or forms. Each Symbol can act as standard lamp or desk light.

For de Castelbajac, light influences perception, just as his fashion garments do. The fertile mind that has given us de Castelbajac-designed tableware, carpets, coffee tables, Swatch watches, graffiti dresses, moonboots and a famous Teddy Bear coat is unlikely to abandon lighting as a medium for creative expression, even if such a busy career means that lighting must share the spotlight with other disciplines.

65

Jean-Charles de Castelbajac

7 symbols series
Crown
Resin, metal
60w bulb
h 36cm l 39cm d 13cm
h 14⅛in l 15⅜in d 5⅛in
Manufacturer
Brossier Saderne, France

66

Enzo
Catellani

Table lamp
Tel Chì
Iron, brass, gold leaf
50w bulb
h 40cm w 50cm l 50cm
h 15¾in w 19⅝in l 19⅝in
Manufacturer
Catellani & Smith srl, Italy

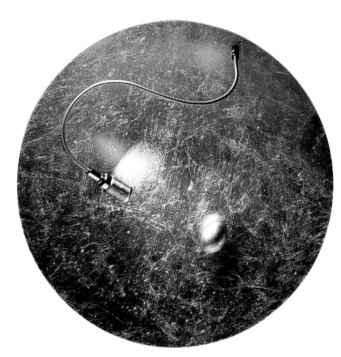

67

Sergio
Calatroni

Table lamp
Narciso
Plastic, rubber, iron
h 25cm di of base 16cm
h 9⅞in di of base 6½in
Prototype
Manufacturer
Afro City Edition, Italy

67

68

Masafumi
Katsukawa

Table lamp
Can Can Qu
Copper-plated metal
20w 12v halogen bulb
h 55cm di 12cm
h 21⅝in di 4¾in
Prototype

69

Antonio
Annicchiarico

Wall light
Chiarina
Perforated chrome-plated metal, ceramic
Max. 100w bulb
h 45cm
h 17¾in
Manufacturer
Quattrifolio, Italy

70

Jorge Garcia
Garay

Ceiling light
Solaris
Metal, crystal
R7S bulb
d 13cm di 38cm
d 5⅛in di 15in
Manufacturer
Garcia Garay SL, Spain

70

68

69

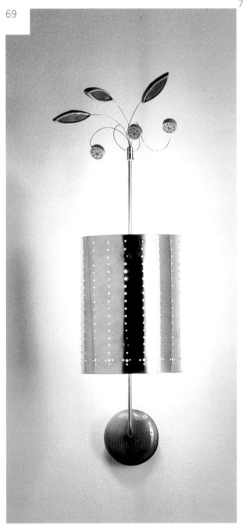

71

71

Stiletto

Table lamp
Pflanzlicht
Terracotta flowerpot
25w green bulb
h 18cm di 11cm
h 7in di 4⅜in
Manufacturer
Koziol, Germany

72

73

72

Michael
Ramharter

Suspension light
Russischer Lüstling
Cloth shades
24 x 25w 220v bulbs
l 150cm di 40–50cm
l 59in di 15¾–19⅝in
Manufacturer
di'(sain) Hagn & Kubala OEG, Austria

73

Louis
Lara

Table lamp
Maya
Steel wire, parafin-coated paper
Compact fluorescent or 40w incandescent bulb
h 61cm w 15cm d 15cm
h 24in w 6in d 6in
Manufacturer
Dansk Lights Inc., USA

74

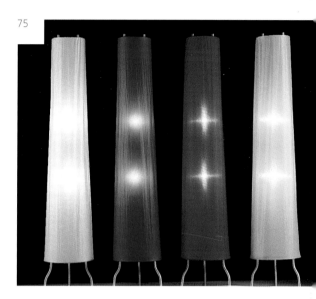

75

74

***Laura*
Kohler*

Suspension light
Lox Lampshades
Wire, paper
60w 110/240v bulb
l 60cm di 60cm
l 23⅝in di 23⅝in
Limited batch production
Manufacturer
SKK Lighting, UK

75

***Rätus*
Wetter*

Standard lamp
Wetter-Leuchte
Powder-coated steel
2 x 60w 220v bulbs
h 160cm di 22–32cm
h 63in di 8⅝in–12⅝in
Manufacturer
di'(sain) Hagn & Kubala OEG, Austria

76
Weyers & Borms

Chandelier
Bruno
Iron, wood, polyester
75w 230v deluxe halogen bulb,
1 top mirror 100w bulb and
1 60w standard filament bulb
h 150cm w 80cm l 400cm
h 59 in w 31 ½ in l 157 ½ in
One-off
Manufacturer
            Weyers & Borms, Belgium

77

Weyers & Borms

Bar light
Flying Fisherman's Friend
Wood, leather, motor, brass, polyester
25w 240v standard yellow bulb and
15w 240v standard bulb
h 40cm w 60cm l 70cm
h 14¾in w 23⅝in l 27½in
One-off
Manufacturer
Weyers & Borms, Belgium

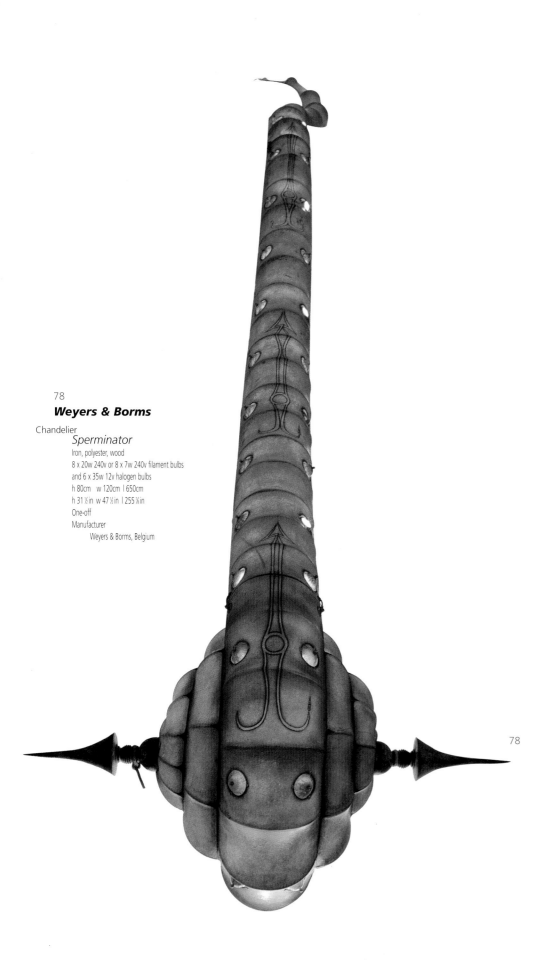

78
Weyers & Borms

Chandelier
Sperminator
Iron, polyester, wood
8 x 20w 240v or 8 x 7w 240v filament bulbs
and 6 x 35w 12v halogen bulbs
h 80cm   w 120cm   l 650cm
h 31 ½ in w 47 ½ in l 255 ⅞ in
One-off
Manufacturer
    Weyers & Borms, Belgium

78

79

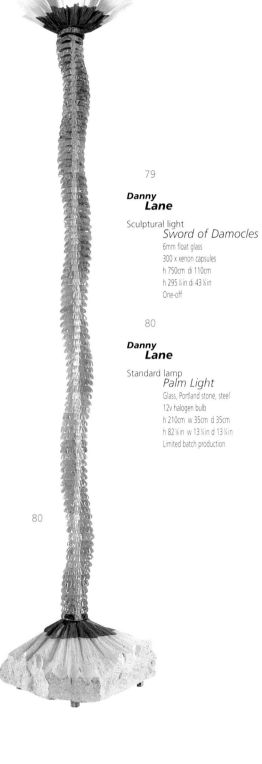

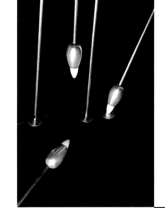

79

Danny
Lane

Sculptural light
Sword of Damocles
6mm float glass
300 x xenon capsules
h 750cm di 110cm
h 295 ¼in di 43 ⅛in
One-off

80

Danny
Lane

Standard lamp
Palm Light
Glass, Portland stone, steel
12v halogen bulb
h 210cm w 35cm d 35cm
h 82 ⅝in w 13 ⅞in d 13 ¾in
Limited batch production

81

Denis
Santachiara

Standard lamp/wall light
Sparta
Aluminium
60w incandescent bulb
h 188cm w 6.5cm
h 74in w 2 ½in
Manufacturer
Oceano Oltreluce, Italy

80

81

Bally Shoe Store

Cologne, Germany
Designer
Ecart

The Cologne store of the Bally chain was designed by Andrée Putman of Ecart to be the high-style flagship of a new worldwide look for the shoe retailer. Warm tones, smooth surfaces, contrasting materials and spiral forms predominate in a retail interior that uses direct and indirect light in an often teasing and playful way. Ecart's pinkish, spiral-form ceiling lights, custom-produced by the German company Megalit (now owned by the Italian Artemide group), are among its most distinctive decorative elements. These fittings, which are made of resin and reflect the form of the helical walnut and metallic-mesh shoe displays below, cast an indirect, opalescent glow over the store.

Elsewhere, low-voltage halogen ceiling spots provide a direct, sparkling display light, while a luminous staircase with sand-blasted glass panels provides the perfect ground-floor setting for a parade of boots and shoes. Bally has not rolled out the new look across its international stores as originally intended. The jewel-like quality of the 300-square-metre interior perhaps defies mass implementation. Nevertheless, Ecart's familiar trademark is present – a relaxed elegance achieved with an economy of means, in which lighting plays a fundamental role.

Left
View through the main
entrance into the Bally Shoe
Store in Cologne. The lighting
plays an important role in
Ecart's retail interior.

Right
A spiral-form ceiling light in
pinkish resin, made by Megalit,
mirrors the shoe display below.
Illuminated sand-blasted glass
panels in the staircase allow
a theatrical display of the
merchandise.

Entel Tower

Santiago, Chile
Designer
Paul Gregory,
Focus Lighting

The spectacularly colourful lighting of the Entel Tower was designed by Paul Gregory of New York-based Focus Lighting for a Chilean telecommunications company which was about to lose its state monopoly and was keen to stay in the public eye. Faced with deregulation, Entel Chile decided to turn its landmark 415-foot tower into a giant advertisement, a glowing beacon of colour, to market its services. This bold idea has been highly successful.

Gregory, who is best known for lighting the disco scenes in the film *Saturday Night Fever* and the Planet Hollywood restaurant interiors, used six motorized 7-kilowatt Xenon searchlights at the very top of the 45-storey tower to emphasize its height. A motorized motion control moves the searchlights every two minutes. The upper, ringed platforms are lit by HID metal-halide lamps used with custom glass colour filters. The square, lower portion of the building is lit by a total of 80 new *AR500* exterior luminaires, made by Irideon (see page 135). These luminaires have computer-controlled dichroic filters that change colours every 20 minutes. This theatrical scheme in downtown Santiago, achieved within severe time constraints, marks the height of technical accomplishment and is clearly visible ten miles away.

Examples of the different colours achieved by Paul Gregory of Focus Lighting in lighting the Entel Tower in Santiago. The balance between the colour-creating Irideon luminaires, which light the lower portion of the building, and the HID metal-halide lamps which light the upper-ring platforms, was achieved by creating a full-scale mockup on a New York church and viewing the results from across the Hudson River.

Casino Magic
Biloxi, Mississippi, USA
Designer
Gallegos Lighting Design

This Gulf Coast casino has been lit in a dramatic and sensual way without resorting to Las Vegas neon in the exterior treatment. Lighting designer Gallegos worked alongside architect Lund & Associates on the casino restoration, combining existing light source technology with cutting-edge fixtures to develop a simple, flexible and eye-catching scheme. A porte-cochere of translucent fabric is underlit with 650-watt halogen lamps covered with custom dichroic colour filters. Two independently controlled colours are used in a programme to allow sweeping colour changes across the translucent canopy, which provides the main lighting under the porte-cochere at the casino entrance.

Additional halogen floods provide focal accents on the elevator and escalator paths to the casino, while metal-halide downlights supply functional lighting for cars dropping off and picking up gamblers. Computer-programmed architectural floodlighting illuminates the casino's towers and planes, which feature kinetic colour transitions. This is a scheme that relies on subtle flourishes of choreographed colour to make its presence felt. Casino Biloxi marks a major lighting advance in a leisure sector best known for dazzling kitsch.

Left
At the entrance to the Casino, the translucent fabric porte-cochere is underlit with 80 650-watt halogen floods with two-colour custom dichroic filters from Orgatek. Additional 1,000-watt Par 64 lamps with coloured glass create focal accents on the escalator and elevator entry paths to the casino. Metal-halide downlights are also part of the scheme.

Below and far left
Exterior views of the casino show the building washed with changing colours. This was achieved by using MSD 700 short-arc metal-halide lamps in programmable floodlights from Irideon.

Main Hall of the City Theatre De Harmonie

Leeuwarden, The Netherlands
Designer
Hans Wolff

Frits van Dongen, architect of the City Theatre De Harmonie, worked closely with lighting designer Hans Wolff to ensure that light plays a prominent role in the building's keen sense of theatricality and illusion. This 12,000-square-metre canal-side municipal theatre in the Dutch town of Leeuwarden has a semi-transparent façade of frosted glass which is perforated in places to make interior shadows and silhouettes clearly visible to passers-by.

The theatre has three vertically-stepped auditoria, with the spaces beneath each serving as dynamic public foyers. All areas expertly harmonize colour, light and texture within tight cost constraints, but perhaps the most innovative lighting is to be found in the main hall. This seats 920 and has a classical plan realized in a highly contemporary way. The balcony is presented as a smooth, elongated teardrop covered in white stucco, while sand-blasted acoustic reflectors attached to the wall in seemingly random fashion conceal dimmable lamps; these provide the auditorium with decorative lighting. Additionally, PAR 64 spotlights create functional but atmospheric light from a lighting bridge. Overall, the lighting of the theatre's spaces achieves a beguiling combination of intimacy and glamour.

Dimmable incandescent lamps concealed behind sand-blasted acoustic reflectors create an ethereal atmosphere in the main auditorium of the City Theatre De Harmonie. Par 64 theatre spotlights provide general lighting.

Peak Health Club
London, UK
Designer
Lighting Design Limited

Above
View of the bar-restaurant area at night. Spiked spotlights from Light Projects send beams of light up the palms in the main lounge. Concord projectors cast dappled patterns over the seating.

Right
Decorative custom-made ceiling bowls in the gymnasium, made by Chelsom, remind keep-fit fanatics that they are still in a hotel.

Far right
To compensate for the lack of a swimming pool, a turquoise neon-lit bar, achieved by lighting cool cathode behind toughened etched-glass panels, gives a feeling of water and health.

Hotel health clubs are tough interiors to design. They need to reconcile a hospitable ambience with the clinical atmosphere associated with fitness. The Peak Health Club, situated on the ninth and tenth floors of the Hyatt Carlton Tower, a hotel just off London's fashionable Sloane Street, uses a combination of decorative and contract lighting to achieve that delicate balance. Lighting consultants Lighting Design Limited worked with interior designers Hirsch Bedner Associates and architect DMWR on the club's refurbishment. Health facilities were relocated to the larger tenth floor and a bar-restaurant sited in the smaller space below. An expanse of glazed façade sends natural daylight flooding into the club from two sides.

On entering the club, a richly illuminated turquoise bar, with etched-glass panels backlit in neon, gives the effect of water and compensates for the lack of a swimming pool. Downlights along an inner curved wall and decorative David Hunt table lamps add to the warmth of the bar-restaurant, while cooler beams of spotlight shoot up palm trees, and Concord's Control Spot system sends dappled patterns through the space. Upstairs in the fitness area, Erco's double focus downlights provide a clinical feel. But the atmosphere is softened by large, yellow, custom-made Chelsom glass domes, reminding guests that they are still in a hotel. The entire scheme on both floors is orchestrated by a Lutron Aurora computer-controlled system, with five presets.

Seattle has a growing reputation as a hotbed of retail marketing trends. This scheme introduces a concept described as 'bagel theatre'. In a bagel bakery/café interior, architects and lighting designers Rik Adams and Rick Mohler have created a visually arresting environment which makes a virtue out of a major structural column in the centre of the 1,400-square-foot space. This column is converted into a decorative lighting fixture, spiralling outwards from the centre. Bowed sheets of galvanized metal attached to the column are lit from within by continuous fluorescent strips. Other fluorescent fittings mounted on black-painted fibreboard provide general lighting and highlighting.

Beneath the spiral, each of the Bagel Bakery's six custom tables is lit by a retro, cable-suspended luminaire: this consists of a standard lava lamp fitted with metal supporting brackets and shade, with a tungsten halogen lamp to moodily light the table below. Low-voltage track lighting highlights the sales counter, menu and product display area. Recessed compact fluorescents illuminate dark walls covered with abstract prehistoric and futuristic images. The overall impression, with the baking and boiling activities of the bagel kitchen open to view, is of quirky individuality – a welcome antidote to the visual blandness of many retail/café design concepts.

SPoT Bagel Bakery

Seattle, Washington, USA

Designer

Adams/Mohler Architects

Left

The lighting of this compact bagel bakery spirals out from a major structural column in the centre of the space, designed as a decorative lighting fixture and lit from within by continuous fluorescent tubes. The six tables are lit by standard kinetic lava lamps attached to custom luminaires.

Below

The servery of the bagel bakery is lit by low-voltage track lighting, while Lightolier recessed compact fluorescents illuminate abstract murals on dark walls.

Grand Harbour Hotel
Southampton, UK
Designer
Maurice Brill Lighting Design

De Vere's Grand Harbour Hotel at Southampton sits close to a major road handling cross-channel ferry traffic. Lighting consultants Maurice Brill Lighting Design determined that this location offered an ideal opportunity to advertise the hotel and entice people inside. The fundamental approach was to project the inner warmth of the hotel, by using cool colour temperatures on the transparent structure of the external façade, and thus allow the inherent warmth of the interior tungsten glow to form a strong contrast. This effect was enhanced by the use of colour and gobo projection, adding a theatrical and decorative dimension to the building.

An array of different luminaires achieve the powerful exterior lighting effects, including a recessed Lucent Lighting uplighter with a blue compact-fluorescent lamp which creates a blue uplight wash at the apex of the central spaceframe. Exterior lighting is similarly carefully planned, with a range of surface- and spike-mounted fittings, and pavement bollards. Internal public spaces have changing light 'scenes' through the day and evening. This is a scheme in which the contrasting aesthetics of the building's modern architectural form and more traditional interiors are skilfully bridged by the use of light.

Top left

Around the main porte-cochere of the Grand Harbour Hotel a warm ambience is created using a tungsten halogen surface-mounted projector from Lightscape Projects.

Left

Lighting of the main swimming pool and whirlpool inside the hotel includes a custom-designed column-mounted uplighter and a cold cathode within the ceiling trough detail.

Right

Exterior view into the Wintergarden area of the hotel. A recessed Lucent Lighting uplighter with a blue compact-fluorescent lamp is built into the central canopy to create a blue wash at the apex of the central spaceframe.

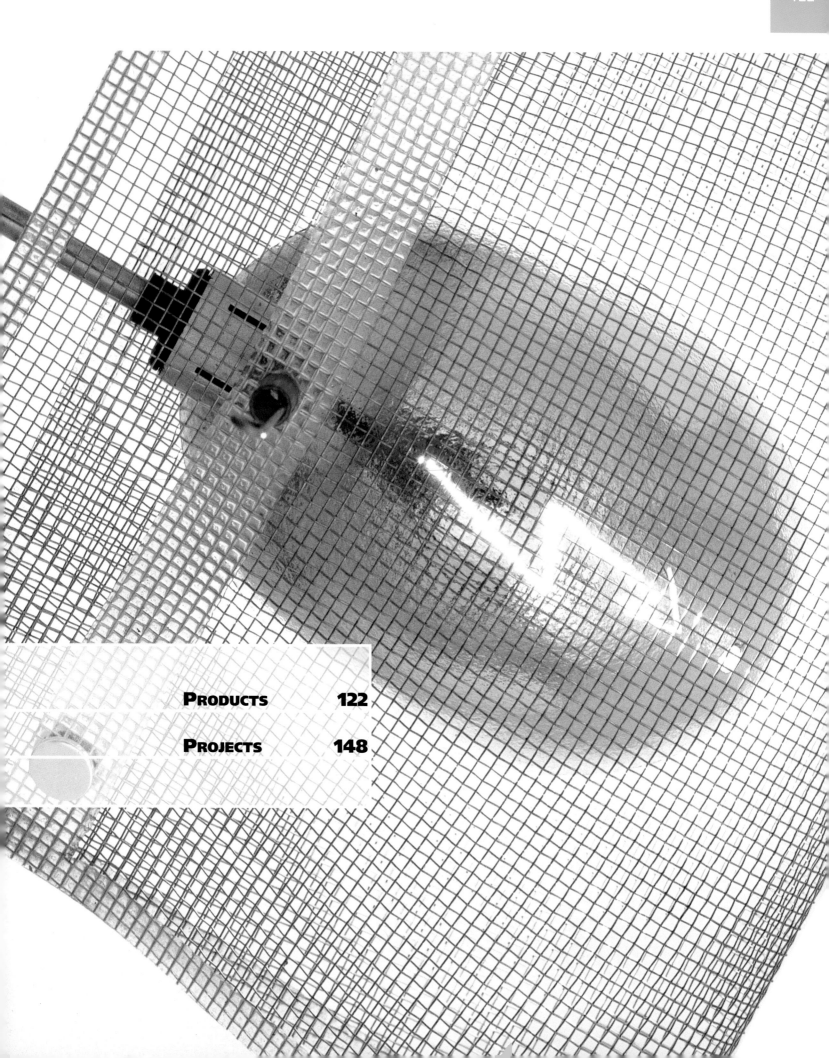

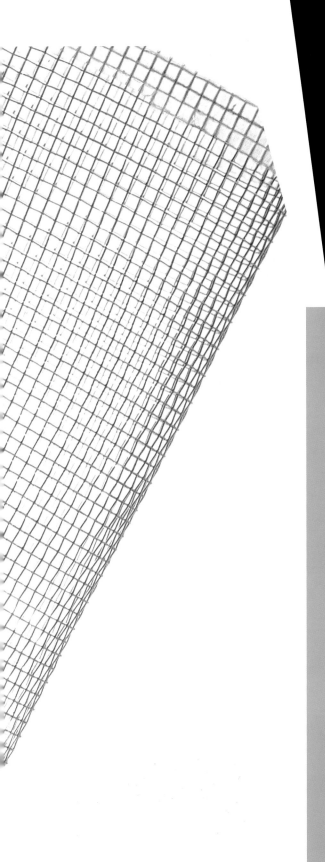

Tailored to the Task

This final section looks at lighting products and systems that carry out tasks in the most effective and imaginative ways possible, and at projects that embody the idea of lighting being fit for a special purpose.

The task lights, work and desk lights, specialist outdoor and display lighting, track and projection systems shown here fulfil a wide variety of tasks – from lighting computer work at a desk to spanning space within a showroom. Function is an essential part of the story, but the sensual solutions often achieved suggest that lighting can be tailored to the task without the need for dogmatic functionalism.

Nobody embodies this idea

more successfully than the Danish designer Knud Holscher whose organic Scandinavian approach lends humanity to the steel-edged qualities of Germany's Erco Lighting. The other light fitting designers profiled here similarly reflect this sense of 'the poetry of the machine' in the way in which they reconcile technical demands with the human experience of the user.

The selection of projects reveals lighting design schemes that are tailored to their task in the most accomplished way possible – from the simulation of soft sunlight in an enclosed gallery of Mexican sculpture at the British Museum to the evocative exterior lighting of a honey-textured Spanish Colonial courthouse in California.

2

1
(Pages 122–3)

Ingo
Maurer

See page 128

2

Isao
Hosoe

Desk light
Tori
Methacrylate, zinc alloy
75w 12v dichroic bulb
h 27cm l 72cm di 17cm
h 10⅝in l 28⅜in di 6⅝in
Manufacturer
Status, Italy

3

3

3

Isao
Hosoe

Desk light
Heron
Reinforced fibreglass
50w 12v halogen bulb
h 64/37cm w 17/9cm l 80cm
h 25⅛/14½in w 6⅜/3½in l 31½in
Manufacturer
Luxo Italiana, Italy

4

4

**Frans van Nieuwenborg &
Martijn Wegman**

Desk light
Radius 1
Extruded aluminium, plastic
50w 12v halogen bulb
h 108cm w 23cm
h 42 ½ in w 9in
Manufacturer
Prandina srl, Italy

5

Rudolf Czapek

Standard lamp
Swandance
Brass or chrome, glass
50w 12v bulb
h 130cm w 120cm
h 51 ⅛ in w 47 ¼ in
Manufacturer
Guardi, Austria

6

**Michele de Lucchi
and Giancarlo Fassina**

Spotlight
Tolomeo Pinza
Polished and anodized aluminium, steel
Max. 100w incandescent bulb
h 23cm w 18cm
h 9in w 7in
Manufacturer
Artemide SpA, Italy

7

Alfonso Milà

Miguel Milà

Federico Correa

Desk light
Diana
Metal, cardboard
2 x 60w bulbs
h 40cm di 46cm
h 15 ¾ in di 18 ⅛ in
Manufacturer
Santa Cole, Ediciones de Diseño SA, Spain

8

Andrée Putman

Desk light
Compas dans l'Oeil
Paper, nickel-plated metal
60w bulb
h 53cm w 19cm d 30cm
h 20 ⅛ in w 7 ½ in d 11 ¾ in
Manufacturer
Ecart SA, France

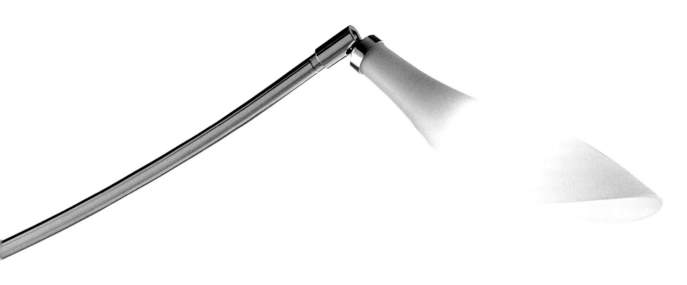

6

7

8

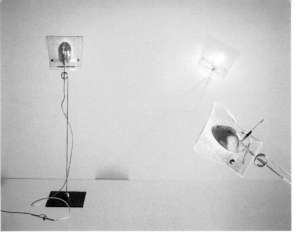

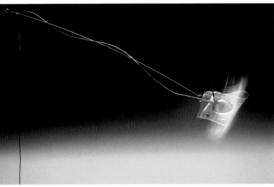

9

Ingo Maurer

Table/wall/clip light
Los Minimalos
Aluminium, steel
50w bulb
h 45cm w 8cm d 5.5cm
h 17⅞in w 3⅛in d 2⅛in
Limited batch production
Manufacturer
Ingo Maurer GmbH, Germany

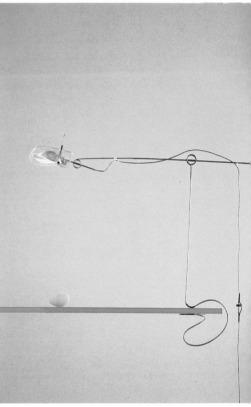

9

Shiu-Kay Kan

Shiu-Kay Kan is a lighting polymath whose activites span the whole spectrum from designing and manufacturing fittings to retailing and architectural lighting consultancy. Since he first emerged on to the London design scene more than 20 years ago with his *Kite Light* for Terence Conran, this Hong Kong-born design entrepreneur has always been at the forefront of new ideas in lighting. His consultancy SKK was started in 1979 and has built a reputation for often quirky invention. But such has been the sheer variety and scope of his work – from the world's first motorized robotic lights which crawl on high-tension wires across the ceiling, to external lighting for the culturally sensitive Grand Buildings development in Trafalgar Square – that he has sometimes been hard to categorize.

The strongest clue to a restless personality lies in Shiu-Kay Kan's background. He trained as an architect in London, including a year at the influential Architectural Association, before taking design jobs with both Norman Foster and Fiorucci. But since going it alone in the late 1970s with garage manufacture of his own lighting products, he has shown most interest in what the latest electronics can do for lighting. He is currently working on a new generation of robot lights that can travel round corners, for the reception area of the sci-fi television channel Science TV. He is also developing lighting ideas for new branches of Cyberia, the on-line café, in Manchester and Tokyo.

But Shiu-Kay Kan is not just interested in technology for its own sake. The presence of a retail showroom in London's Soho reflects a role in the softer, domestic side of lighting. 'We put a prototype in the window for two weeks and if the public responds well, we manufacture it. I tell my designers not to think of my taste but of customers,' he explains. His *Techno Mantis* task light, shown here, is a good example of his approach of making people curious about lighting. 'It is a table light for young children to assemble themselves and do their homework by. It is an inexpensive, fun product that draws on Techno music and the idea of the Internet as a spider in a web.' Currently, however, his greatest enthusiasm is for kinetic lighting. 'Lights which have movement – water bubble, projector or robot lights, using motors or heat or colours – are so attractive to people. That's the direction we are now pushing.'

10

10

**Shiu-Kay
Kan**

Desk light
Techno Mantis
Zinc-plated steel, rubber
Max. 40w 240v bulb
h 13cm
h 5⅛in
Manufacturer
SKK Lighting, UK

11

Sergio Asti

and Inao Miura

Desk light and standard lamp
Kirin
Metal
50w halogen bulb
Standard lamp: h 115cm w 100cm
h 45¼ in w 39⅜ in
Desk light: h 70cm w 80cm
h 27½ in w 31½ in
Manufacturer
Fantasy for Light, Italy

11

12

Jordi Vilardell
Iglesias

Desk light/standard lamp
Sister
Injected polycarbonate
Standard lamp: h 135cm w 23cm d 25cm
h 53 ⅛in w 9in d 9 ⅞in
Desk light: h 45cm w 23cm d 17cm
h 17 ¾in w 9in d 6 ⅝in
Manufacturer
 Gargot Disseny Mediterrani SA, Spain

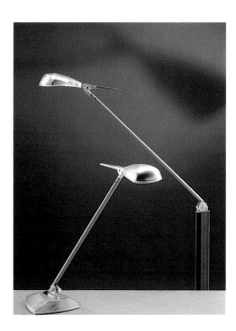

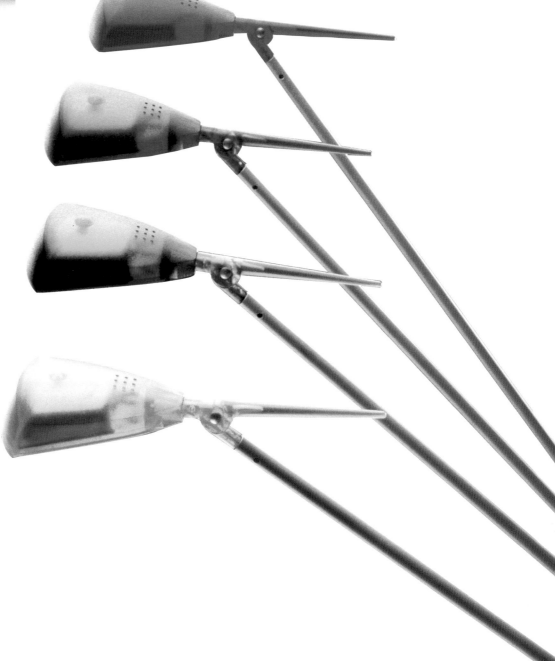

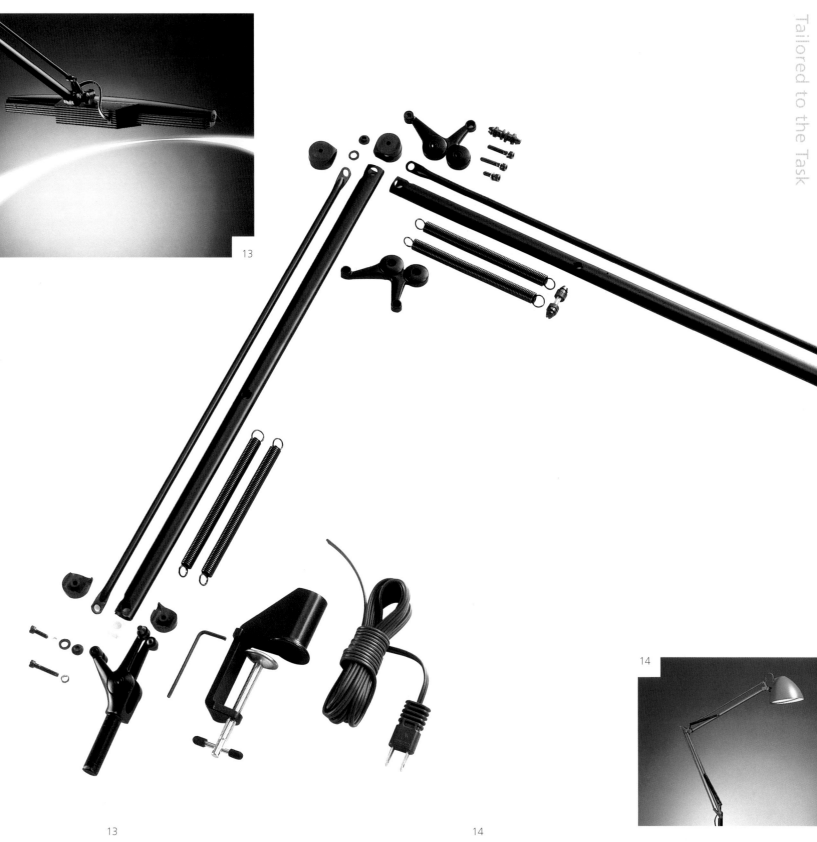

13

14

13

Sigeaki
Asahara

Desk light
Z-999
Metal, plastic
27w neon bulb
h 43cm w 47cm l 56cm
h 16⅞in w 18½in l 22in
Manufacturer
Yamada Shoumei, Japan

14

Sigeaki
Asahara

Desk light
Z-901
Aluminium
60w PS krypton bulb
h 94.5cm w 62cm
h 37in w 24⅜in
Manufacturer
Yamada Shoumei, Japan

Profile

Sigeaki *Asahara*

Sigeaki Asahara originally wanted to be a sculptor and travelled from Japan to Turin to study sculpture at the age of 17. This background is reflected in his lighting products which combine a European sensibility towards form with an Oriental affinity for functional light. Asahara stayed on in Italy to work in an architectural office and became a designer of furniture, tableware and other household products. But it is lighting that especially captures his interest. He works for both western and eastern companies and could be said to occupy a pivotal position between two distinct lighting cultures.

'The way of thinking about lighting in Europe is quite different to the Japanese,' explains Asahara. He describes a contrast between brick or stone European homes, with comparatively small windows and quite dark interiors even during daylight, and Japanese houses with huge windows on two or three sides of a room to let in a wash of sunlight. Cultural and climatic differences mean that Europeans are more keen on indirect wall lights, standard lamps and spotlights to make their spaces cosy and interesting, whereas at night the Japanese simply want the functional replacement of daylight in a room.

Asahara's own portfolio reflects the cultural divisions between west and east in lighting. Among his soft and attractive designs for Italian manufacturer Lucitalia is a wood and die-cast aluminium standard lamp called *Mehnir*, a glowing ceiling light called *Olla*, and a focus-adjustable range of spotlights called *Kri* (see pages 17, 96 and 144–5). Each piece shows a sculptural finesse – the *Kri* spotlights in particular suggest a jeweller's eye for detail – without forgetting the task in hand. Function is a key part of Japanese lighting, and Asahara's table lamps for the Japanese company Yamada Shoumei are elegant refinements of the traditional jointed-arm task light, with special reflectors that ensure users are not blinded by glare.

Japanese commissions, says Asahara, tend to be tailored to specific user needs, in the office or study for example, whereas in Italy he is not·constrained by specific requirements and is freer to use his imagination to create lighting for others to use in their own way. For inspiration he looks to the old things of Europe – buildings, furniture and artefacts that people have cherished for centuries. This is perhaps another link with his early cultural bent towards sculpture.

15

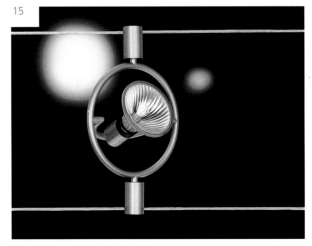

15

Franco
Bettonica

and Mario
Melocchi

Lighting system
Tenso 2500W
Steel cable
Max. 150w bulb
l 300cm
l 118½ in
Manufacturer
Cini & Nils, Italy

16

16

Perry A.
King
and Santiago
Miranda

with Malcolm S. Inglis
Bollard light
Borealis
Die-cast aluminium, opal polycarbonate
50 HQL–100w INC and 26w TC-T–50w MH
h 115cm di 30cm
h 45 ¼in di 11 ¾in
Manufacturer
Louis Poulsen, Denmark

17
Irideon Ltd

Exterior floodlight
Irideon AR500
Cast aluminium
700w MSD bulb
h 70cm w 68cm l 58cm
h 27 ½ in w 26 ¾ in l 22 ¾ in
Manufacturer
Irideon Ltd, UK

18

Targetti
Design

Precision directional downlight
Mondial
Diecast aluminium
Metal halide, halospot 111, halogen H1-P24 bulbs
h 9–17cm di 12–20cm
h 3 ½–6 ⅝in di 4 ¼–7 ⅞in
Manufacturer
    Targetti Sankey SpA, Italy

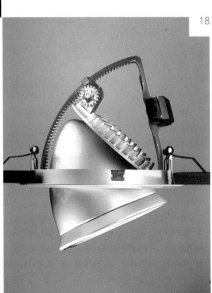

18

19

Perry A.
King

and Santiago
Miranda

Architectural lighting
Lucille
Metal, plastic
Low-voltage halogen bulb
h 13.5/9.5cm di 11.5/8.5cm
h 5 ¼/3 ¾ in di 4 ½/3 ⅜ in
Manufacturer
Flight (Division of Flos SpA), Italy

20

Friedbert
Meinert

Spotlight
PAR 30
Aluminium
75/100w 240v bulb
h 18cm w 13cm l 13cm
h 7in w 5 ⅛in l 5 ⅛in
Manufacturer
	Basis Design Limited, UK

21

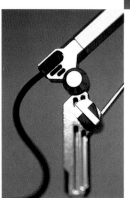

22

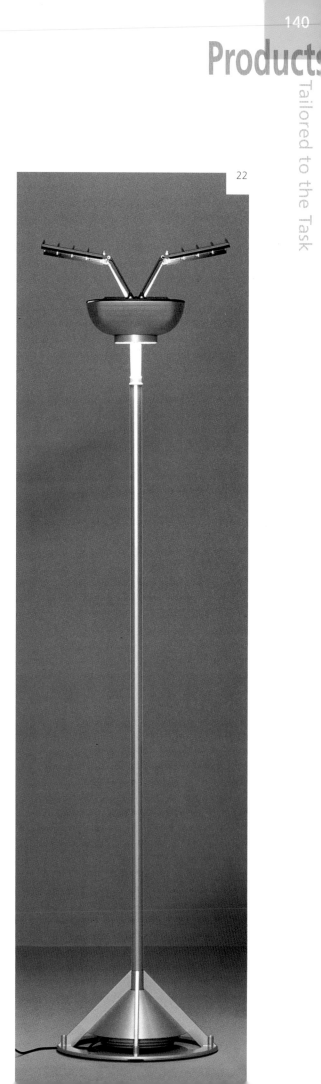

21

**Franco
Clivio**

Desk light
Lucy
Solid cast aluminium, plastic
18/50w 12v low voltage halogen bulb
(small head)
Compact fluorescent (large head)
h 180cm di 30cm
h 70⅞in di 11¾in
Manufacturer
     Erco Leuchten GmbH, Germany

Knud *Holscher*

Veteran Danish designer and architect Knud Holscher belongs to the living tradition of Scandinavian Modernism which reached its peak of popularity in the 1950s and 1960s, at a time when Holscher worked as Arne Jacobsen's architectural associate on St Catherine's College, Oxford. More than 30 years later, Holscher has managed to remain relevant to contemporary audiences without sacrificing his design principles. His products reflect the virtues of clarity, honesty, simplicity and precision which are essential to modern Danish design. It is a philosophy the writer Kim Dirckinck-Holmfeld has described as embodying 'the poetry of moderation'. A 'moderate Modernist' would sum up Holscher especially well in the field of lighting where he has developed a close relationship in the 1990s with German lighting company Erco.

23

Holscher has brought a more humanistic sense of form to Erco's serious technical approach, lending credence to his claim that despite being a former assistant to Jacobsen and a former professor in the architectural school of Copenhagen's Royal Academy of Arts, he is 'no dyed-in-the-wool functionalist'. His first project with Erco was the *Quinta* range of spotlights launched in 1993, with its ribbing evocative of a sea shell. Following *Quinta*'s commercial success, Holscher worked on a second Erco project: a silver uplighting system called *Zenit*, designed to work in tandem with another new Erco system – Franco Clivio's *Lucy* task light range – to achieve a balance between task and general lighting for computer workers in offices. *Zenit* has wing-like reflector elements which cast some light on to the work surface, where it is supplemented by *Lucy*'s compact-fluorescent lighting, but most on to the ceiling to create comfortable, dazzle-free general lighting.

22

Knud
Holscher

Standard lamp
Zenit
Aluminium, frosted glass
70/150/250w halogen bulb
h 185cm di 25.2cm
h 72 ⅞in di 9 ⅞in
Manufacturer
Erco Leuchten GmbH, Germany

23

Knud
Holscher

Spotlight
Quinta
Manufacturer
Erco Leuchten GmbH, Germany

Holscher, who worked entirely separately from Clivio, claims it is a simple, integrated solution to a very complex problem. But then finding such answers has been a keynote of his career, from his tableware for Georg Jensen and his best-selling D-Line architectural fittings for Carl F. Petersen to his remodelling of Copenhagen Airport in 1986 and his Danish Pavilion, with its sail-like forms, for the 1992 Seville World Expo.

At 65, Knud Holscher is still full of ideas. He recently left a large architectural practice to set up his own design office and is currently working on station designs for Copenhagen's S-train underground system. Lighting remains a preoccupation for this modest master. He is collaborating with Austrian lighting consultant Christian Bartenbach, and he eagerly awaits Erco's next call.

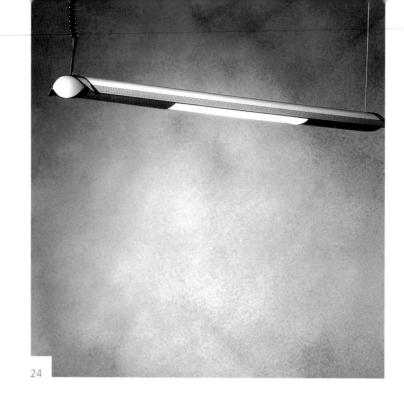

24

Koen
de Winter

Pendant
Winglite
Coated aluminium, acrylic, glass
High-efficiency compact fluorescent
h 6cm w 20cm l 126/188cm
h 2½in w 7⅞in l 49½/74in
Manufacturer
    Axis Lighting, Canada

24

25

Massimo
Sacconi

Pendant
Flap Plus
Aluminium, steel
70–150w metal-halide bulbs
h 65cm w 29cm l 73cm
h 25⅝in w 11⅜in l 28¾in
One-off
Manufacturer
    Nordlight SpA, Italy

25

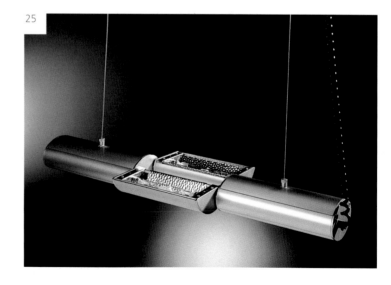

Tobias
Grau

Spotlight
Name
Plastic, bronze, aluminium
105w low-voltage halogen bulb
h 14cm di 36cm
h 5½in di 14⅛in
Manufacturer
Tobias Grau KG GmbH & Co., Germany

27

Tobias
Grau

Lighting system
Name
Plastic, bronze, aluminium
Two-phase low-voltage halogen bulb
h 20cm l variable, max. 250cm
h 7⅞in l variable, max. 98⅜in
Manufacturer
Tobias Grau KG GmbH & Co., Germany

27

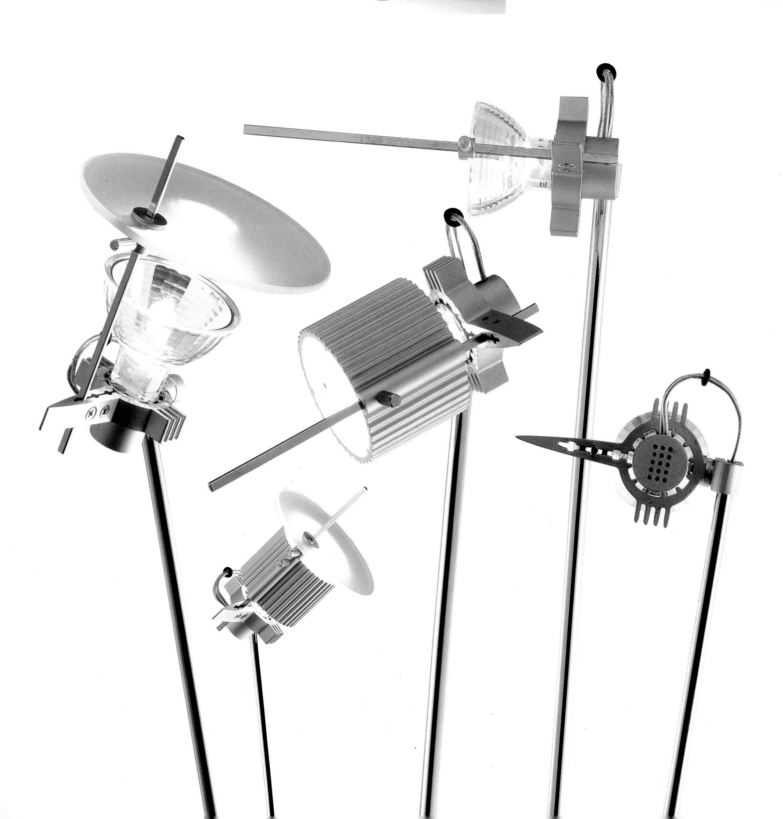

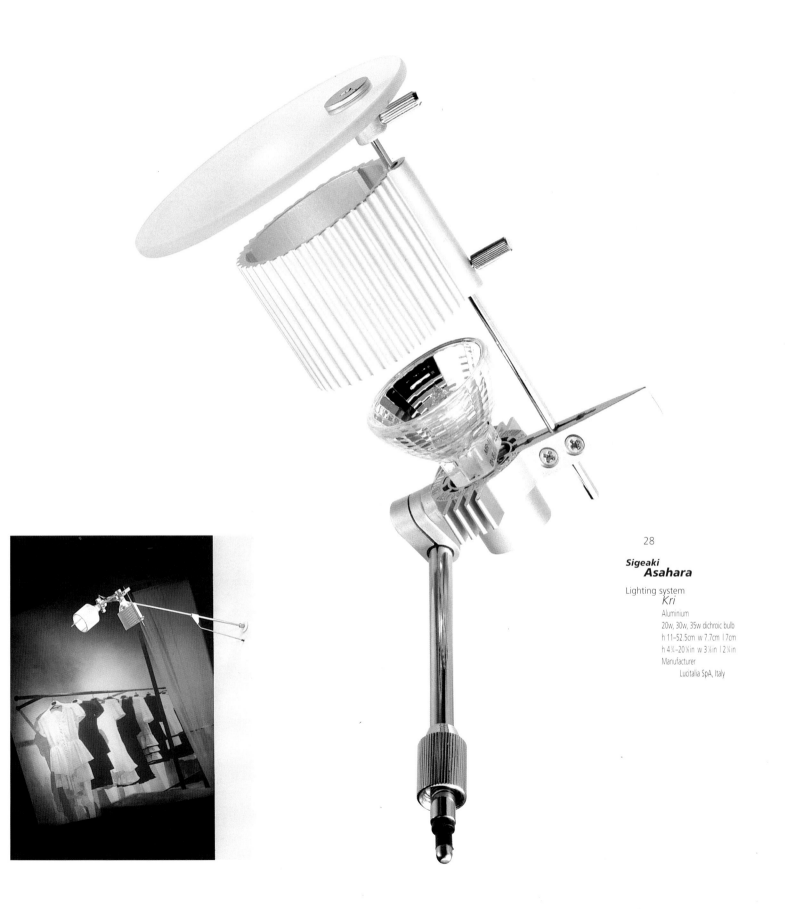

28

Sigeaki
Asahara

Lighting system
Kri
Aluminium
20w, 30w, 35w dichroic bulb
h 11–52.5cm w 7.7cm l 7cm
h 4¾–20⅝in w 3⅛in l 2¾in
Manufacturer
Lucitalia SpA, Italy

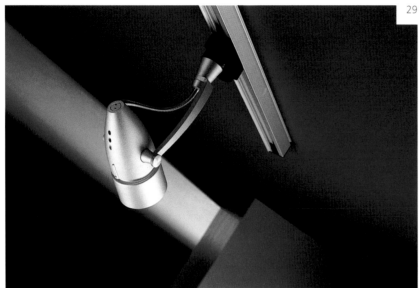

29

29

Hannes
Wettstein

Lighting system,
CYOS
(Create Your Own System)
Aluminium
Various/max. 230v bulb
h 22.5–30.5cm d 13–24cm
h 8¼–12in d 5⅛–9½in
Manufacturer
        Belux, Switzerland

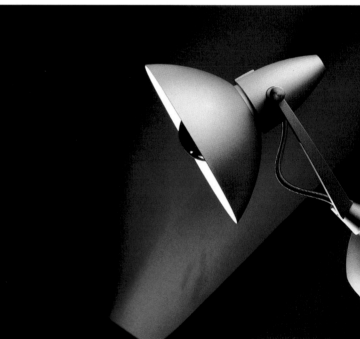

Hannes **Wettstein**

Swiss product designer Hannes Wettstein describes himself as working at 'the margins of architecture and interior design'. In this context, he regards lighting as very important in both defining and changing the characteristics of any given space. Since 1982 Wettstein, who studied architecture and building engineering in Zurich, has enjoyed a relationship with Swiss lighting manufacturer Belux which has given him the creative scope to explore his ideas to the full.

Wettstein began working for Belux on heavy-duty factory lights, but as the manufacturer has gradually turned its attention and investment towards lighting products for home and office, he has been able to widen his repertoire. He claims to have produced the world's first low-voltage halogen lighting system, *Metro*, even ahead of Ingo Maurer, while his *Snodo* work light was an exercise in robust minimalism, and his *Boomerang* system was an early pioneer of mini compact-fluorescent sources.

Wettstein's latest collaboration with Belux is called *CYOS* (which stands for *Create Your Own System*). It is, he declares, 'one economical system for all the different characteristics of light. You just change the lamps and the reflectors to suit your needs.' It is indeed an ingenious solution, with cabling integrated into a minimal system so that the small die-cast aluminium lamp element is fully rotatable. This means you can use colours and lenses to alter the ambience of a home, office or showroom without the aid of tools. The system takes a variety of sources, from bright halogen to compact fluorescent, and can be wall, floor or ceiling mounted. 'I searched for an image to combine private and professional use,' says Wettstein, 'and I thought of the personal camera which is easy to use but reflects professional competence.'

Wettstein's lighting innovation is informed by his interior design work. He is currently working on the Swiss Ambassador's residence in Madrid and with Spanish architect José Rafael Moneo on a hotel in Berlin. His professorial role at the ETH Zurich, the Technical University of Switzerland, and his creative role as a member of the Zed design network, which is currently working on a new lighting range for Artemide, guarantees a busy life. In furniture Wettstein has followed up his 1994 *Bill* sofa system for Baleri with a table system which, he says, 'you can mount in 30 seconds'. Whatever the project, what matters to Wettstein is the user's personal experience.

Mexican Gallery of the British Museum

London, UK

Designer

Fisher Marantz Renfro Stone

Meso-American sculptures originally designed to be seen outside are lit by consultant Paul Marantz in an enclosed gallery, using a custom fitting from Designed Architectural Lighting (DAL) to recreate natural outdoor conditions. To achieve a balance between light which reveals texture, and light which softens shadows, each sculpture is frontlit by a single fitting containing four PAR 36 lamps.

An unprepossessing lower floor cataloguing room in the British Museum has been dramatically transformed by architect Teodoro González de Leon into a rich and sensual gallery to display 180 pieces of meso-American sculpture, including pieces from the Aztec and Mayan eras. The key lighting challenge, as consultant Paul Marantz of Fisher Marantz Renfro Stone explains, was 'to solve the perpetual problem of lighting medium-scale sculpture designed to be seen outdoors in daylight but, as here, displayed in an enclosed gallery'.

Marantz explains that daylight is a combination of sunlight, which produces crisp shadows and reveals texture, and skylight, which is diffuse and softens the shadows. Interior spotlights tend to render objects with more dramatic contrast than the artist intended, but the 187-square metre gallery space gave little opportunity for daylighting. Marantz's solution drew on the example of portrait photographers, who solve similar problems by using a variety of 'softlights', typically white light reflected from white umbrellas or large diffusers.

A new fitting was developed with a face much larger than the normal track light fitting. It contains four 12-volt, 100-watt metal reflector PAR 36 lamps providing a single source of almost 300 square millimetres. Each sculpture is frontlit by a single fitting designed to simulate the sun in providing a coherent system of shadows, but large enough to prevent these shadows from becoming too hard. In addition, display cases are lit by a combination of fibre optics, fluorescent and tungsten halogen.

Reading Rooms of the Biblioteca de Catalunya
Barcelona, Spain
Designer
Joan Rodon and Erco Lighting

Barcelona architect Joan Rodon's skilful restoration of the reading rooms of the Biblioteca de Catalunya marks the first of three planned phases of renovation for this historic building, which dates back to 1401 and was originally Calalonia's largest hospital. Three interconnecting rooms in what is generally regarded as the most beautiful part of the building have been given a contemporary design flavour in a scheme that puts the accent on lighting to suggest a fresh approach.

Rodon, who repaired or replaced the masonry, wooden ceilings and floors, worked with Erco Lighting to develop light solutions. Stone arched buttresses are lit by halogen Eclipse projectors, positioned to be invisible to the observer. Walls lined with wooden bookcases are washed with even, low-voltage halogen light from Compar wallwashers, while track for low-voltage halogen lamps has been installed at the upper level of bookshelves. One particularly innovative feature is the use of recessed luminaires integrated into the reading desks at ankle level to illuminate the circulation areas. A once gloomy interior has a warm new ambience, and an old, crumbling library now has the latest information technology. The Biblioteca de Catalunya has nearly a million books, but most will not be available at this site until a later renovation of a subterranean archive on five floors is complete.

Innovative contemporary lighting is a hallmark of the restoration of the Biblioteca de Catalunya.

Left
Recessed CL luminaires are integrated into the reading desks at ankle level to illuminate circulation areas on the upper floor.

Right
Erco's Compar wallwashers and spotlights sit on Minirail low-voltage track to light bookshelves and reading tables. The stone-arched Gothic vaulting of this beautiful historic building is lit by Eclipse halogen spotlights installed below the corbels and concealed from view behind the shelves.

Belgo Centraal Restaurant
London, UK
Designer
Ron Arad Associates

Above
> The entrance to Belgo Centraal
> is across the illuminated plates
> of a metal bridge open on each
> side to the steaming kitchen
> below.

Right
> View of the main basement
> restaurant space. The low
> vaulted ceiling is left
> deliberately bare, highlighted
> by small low-voltage directional
> spots from Basis Design.

Far right
> Uplighting is incorporated into
> the restaurant banquettes in
> Ron Arad and Alison Brooks'
> design. Light emerges from
> gaps between layers of rolled
> galvanized metal cladding.

After the intimacy of Belgo Noord in Chalk Farm, Ron Arad Associates' second London restaurant for clients Andre Plisnier and Denis Blais – Belgo Centraal in Covent Garden – is on a far larger and more industrial scale. The venue for this Belgian-style eaterie is a vast vaulted warehouse basement. Architects Ron Arad and Alison Brooks have made the entrance to this dark subterranean cavern into a spectacle in its own right. Diners must cross the circular illuminated plates of a metal bridge, with views on each side of a gleaming open kitchen counter dispenser below, and descend into the restaurant via a mesh-clad industrial elevator. This scissor-mechanism lift is backlit with die-cast raw aluminium low-voltage spotlights, using a sandblasted glass diffuser to reduce glare and spread the beam.

Within the restaurant, which seats 275, the aim was to 'keep lights and wires off the low-height vaulted ceilings and make the interior as bare as possible,' explains Alison Brooks. The architects worked with Basis Design to develop a small, low-voltage directional spot to highlight the basement vaults. Uplighting incorporated into custom furniture further raises lux levels and gently washes the vaults with light, while uplighting from below eye level is achieved using sandblasted glass diffusers with dichroic halogen lamps. The contrast of cool, watery colours with richer, more earthy tones is part of the visual blend of the restaurant, which is based on the North European beer hall.

National Museum of Natural History
Paris, France
Designer
René Allio

Beneath a ceiling that functions as an artificial sky, France's famous National Museum of Natural History is back in business. It has been triumphantly restored with dramatic light settings – *scenographie* is the French term – an essential part of the new museum design. Jules André's grand Parisian building was originally acquired for the 1889 World Exhibition. It suffered severe bomb damage in World War Two and was closed for nearly 30 years. But today its renovation by Paul Chemetov and Borja Huidobro has given the public a magnificent main gallery – the Galerie de l'Evolution – in which lighting designer René Allio's lyrical lighting *mise-en-scène* of the exhibits has been highly praised.

As a Noah's Ark of animals parade down the full length of the gallery, they are bathed in light by beams of stage spotlights, like performers in a giant play. The scheme reflects the respect of the renovating architects for the original building. There is no blatant design intervention. The relationship between the central nave and the encircling galleries (with their oak-framed, fibre-optic-lit display cases on three levels) is preserved, so that Allio's lighting creates a giant evolutionary crucible for the creatures to inhabit.

Stage spotlights capture the magic of the natural world in lighting designer René Allio's masterful scenes for the Natural History Museum, Paris. The ceiling of Jule André's grand building is an artificially lit sky; display cabinets are lit with fibre optics.

Birmingham School of Art

Birmingham, UK
Designer
Concord Sylvania

The total refurbishment and partial rebuilding of Birmingham School of Art's neglected Grade 1 listed Victorian building has given a new lease of life to the world's first purpose-built municipal art school. The Gothic-Revival School was originally designed by Chamberlain and Martin in 1885. More than a century later, its principal studio and exhibition spaces have been returned to their original form, with new mezzanine floors added to provide new teaching and office areas in a scheme designed by Associated Architects. New restaurant, library and conference facilities have also been added. Lighting was a key element of the programme. The architects collaborated with Concord Sylvania Specials Department on ways to enhance both the robust character of the original spaces and the new building elements.

Concord Sylvania's solution was a custom-designed linear lighting system in a series of bays. This fitting, made of mild steel and extruded aluminium, houses louvred fluorescents; it provides uplighting as well as downlighting and can also carry track for spotlighting. Its flexibility has enabled sympathetic lighting of the School's studio and public spaces, and its curved profile visually complements the character of the building.

Concord Sylvania's custom-designed linear lighting system, housing louvred fluorescents, complements the Gothic architecture of the refurbished Birmingham School of Art. The flexible and robust system provides facilities for uplighting, downlighting and spotlights.

Above
    A view of the cathedral interior shows the combination of functional high-pressure metal-halide lighting for general illumination across arches and ceilings with more decorative low-voltage dichroic sources and narrow-beam spotlights which accent gilded details.

Right
    The secondary altar lit by specially designed narrow-beam luminaires. All the lighting fixtures are by Reggiani and the light sources are from Osram.

Basilica Nuestra Señora del Pilar

Buenos Aires, Argentina
Designer
Leonor Bedel & Asociados

The soaring arches and gilded decoration of this newly restored Buenos Aires cathedral have been sensitively illuminated in a scheme by Leonor Bedel & Asociados which combines high tech with the holy faith. A place of worship, the cathedral is also famous for its colonial antiques. In response, the designer has combined two different lighting systems, one functional and the other decorative. Direct and indirect high-pressure metal-halide lamps provide general ambient lighting across the arches and ceiling, while full-spectrum low-voltage dichroic sources and narrow-beam spotlights bring out the warmth of the gilded details.

Throughout the scheme, the energy-efficient new lighting technology is fitted unobtrusively into the interior fabric. A computerized system which controls 45 circuits and nine pre-set lighting 'scenes' allows the cathedral to be specially lit for every occasion. The main nave area, a surface of 320 square metres, combines metal halide for general lighting with incandescent chandeliers on each side. Specially designed narrow-beam luminaires light the saintly images situated in between secondary altars on the wall from a distance of 13 metres. The restoration project at the Basilica Nuestra Señora del Pilar was led by architects Pombo & Lamarca.

Bibliothèque Nationale de France

Paris, France
Designer
Gaëlle Lauriot Prévost, Inge Waes for Dominique Perrault

France's new landmark National Library, sited on a stretch of industrial wasteland in the East End of Paris, is based on a simple design metaphor. Its form comprises four giant glass towers shaped like open books. These high-rise structures face each other across a vast rectangular garden plaza, enclosing 12 million books within a glazed treasury, in a scheme described by its architect Dominique Perrault as an attempt to 'rediscover emotions built on paradoxes between presence and absence, the human and monumental, the opaque and luminous'. Light is an essential to Perrault's approach, not simply in the way he uses opaque wooden shutters to shade the glass towers from daylight, but in his lighting of interior spaces, most notably the thematic libraries and archive rooms that surround the sunken garden at the kernel of the project.

The interior lighting scheme designed by Gaëlle Lauriot Prévost and Inge Waes makes use of a number of suppliers, from Erco's spotlighting and Sammode's hanging lights in the conference rooms to a Zumtobel fluorescent lighting system for the underground archives, comprising 15.4 kilometres of track and more than 12,000 special ZX luminaires with Tridonic electronic ballasts. The system meets the safety and conservation standards laid down for environments storing valuable cultural items which are likely to fade under intense light. Overall, the lighting for one of France's most significant *grand projets* enhances the palette of glass, metallic fabric, raw concrete and wood which makes the interiors so distinctive.

Above
Dominique Perrault's Bibliothèque Nationale de France, a study in the contrast between the luminous and the opaque.

Left
Custom-designed lighting in the research reading rooms that wrap around the sunken garden.

Manchester Airport Pedestrian Link
Manchester, UK
Designer
Lighting Design Partnership

Above
External view of the fixed link at night.

Right
Inside the pedestrian link. The artificial lighting automatically responds to changes in the availability of natural light. Colour and kinetic movement are a feature of the scheme's subtly 'rippling' fluorescence. Cold cathode arches signal the approach of the terminal.

A fixed pedestrian causeway at Manchester Airport, which links the main airport terminal with a car park and rail station, has avoided the dull monotony of most passenger tunnels by using an imaginative lighting scheme to enhance the user experience. The colour and kinetic movement of the lighting shortens the visual perception of the 250-metre long link and creates a calming atmosphere inside the highly visible, glass-walled structure.

During the day, the link receives substantial amounts of natural light. When light levels fall, fluorescent lights concealed in perimeter cove details and above a suspended 'ribbon' ceiling are automatically activated. These send a smooth blue wash via custom-designed reflectors through the tube, whilst still allowing external views. Designers Barry Hannaford and Tom Downey have also achieved a sense of movement by subtly 'rippling' the fluorescence in sequence along the length of the structure, using an automated photocell and time-clock process. Custom-designed, compact-fluorescent 'runway' luminaires with blue dichroic glass filters create additional colour variation through the blue/magenta spectrum, while recessed low-voltage downlights in the ceiling add sparkling points of white light along the entire length of the link. The approach of the main terminal is signalled by arches of white cold cathode within architectural details – another flourish in a scheme which marries the technical and aesthetic with great finesse.

Below

The stucco and sandstone façade of the Santa Barbara County Courthouse is warmly washed by high-pressure sodium. The colour rendering accentuates the building's honey-like texture.

Right

Ground-mounted fixtures concealed in low-level planting graze the building with light whilst minimizing shadowing above windows. Palm canopies are highlighted through the use of clear mercury focal lighting.

Santa Barbara County Courthouse
Santa Barbara, California, USA
Designer
Ross De Alessi Lighting Design

Ross De Alessi's evocative exterior lighting has brought a sense
of romance to a fine example of Spanish Colonial architecture
built in the late 1920s. The stucco and sandstone façade of this
historical landmark and working courthouse in Santa Barbara's
business district is revealed in a soft golden light, with all
incandescent lamps dimmed to warm their colour. The rich,
honey-like texture is accentuated by warm washes and grazes
of light in an approach which De Alessi likens to old-style
luminarios.

The designer's concept for a building which makes use of
ceramics, metals and tiles in its features was 'born of fire'. High-
pressure sodium was therefore used to achieve the building's
warm tones. The long-life characteristic of this source was
important given the project's key design requirements:
aesthetics, energy efficiency, ease of maintenance and minimum
penetration of the building fabric. All equipment is unobtrusive.
Ground-mounted fixtures are concealed in low-level planting,
while subtle shadowing of arch and window irregularity at
concealed ledge level emphasizes the building's rather beguiling
asymmetry. This was a project which the courthouse's Board of
Curators initially turned down. But it finally went ahead after
a full site mock-up and won the International Lighting Design
Association's highest honour, the Award of Excellence, in 1995.

Biographies and Company Profiles

Adams/Mohler Architects

is based in Seattle and specializes in architectural services for residential, commercial and institutional clients. The practice was founded in 1991 by Rik Adams and Rick Mohler. Adams has degrees in both Architecture and Fine Arts, while Mohler is a part-time Associate Professor of Architecture at the University of Washington. In 1994 the practice was joined by Rick Ghillino who has over 12 year's experience as a project architect.

Antonio Annicchiarico

was born in Grotteglie in Southern Italy in 1953. He studied engineering and has a degree from the University of Barl but is also interested in ceramic art and architecture. He is the founder of a study group, ARCA, whose main activity is the restoration of a historical building called Casa Mastropaolo. Annicchiarico was amongst the selected architects for the third Mostra Internazionale di Architettura in Venice and in 1986 participated in the International Design Exhibition in Frankfurt with furniture pieces that combined wood and ceramic. Since 1986 he has been involved in cinema and theatre and was art director of the film *Piccolo Diavolo* with Walter Matthau. From 1990 to 1994 he designed several lights and pieces of furniture including the *Luci del Sud* series of lights made of metal and ceramic for Quattrifolio.

Ron Arad

was born in Tel Aviv in 1951 and studied at the Jerusalem Academy of Art and the Architectural Association, London (from 1974 to 1979). In 1981 he founded One Off Ltd with Dennis Groves and Caroline Thorman and in 1983 designed One Off's first showroom in Neal Street, Covent Garden. He started to exhibit both nationally and internationally, as well as hosting shows for other designers, notably Danny Lane, Tom Dixon and Jon Mills in 1986. In 1988 he won the Tel Aviv Opera Foyer Interior Competition with C. Norton

and S. McAdam, and the next year formed Ron Arad Associates in order to realize the project, moving premises to Chalk Farm, London. As well as the design and construction of the new One Off design studio, furniture gallery and workshop in 1990, recent projects have included furniture design for Poltronova, Vitra, Moroso and Driade, the design of various interior installations and domestic architectural projects. Ron Arad was the editor of the 1994 *International Design Yearbook* and is a guest Professor at the University of Applied Arts in Vienna. Exhibitions include 'Breeding in Captivity', a one-man show at the Edward Totah Gallery, London; joint shows with Ingo Maurer at the Galleria Internos and at the Galleria Facsimile, Milan and 'Gaz Naturel, L'Energie Créative' at the Grand Palais, Paris.

Josep Aregall

was born in Barcelona in 1957 and since 1979 has designed and built commercial spaces, houses and offices. He has also designed exhibitions and temporary constructions, and has been Professor of Window Dressing and Temporary Constructions at the EINA Design School since 1985. He collaborated in the Barcelona Cinema Festival in 1987, 1988 and 1990 and the 'EINA-20 Years Exhibition'. He designed the travelling exhibition for the presentation of the 1992 Barcelona Paraolympic Games, as well as collaborating on the interior design for part of the Industry and Energy Pavilion at EXPO'92 in Seville.

Sigeaki Asahara

was born in Tokyo in 1948 and studied in Torino, Italy. Since 1972 he has worked as a freelance industrial designer in Tokyo. He exhibits internationally, and one of his projects is on permanent show at the Brooklyn Museum of New York. His work has received much acclaim including a Compasso d'Oro and the IF Prize at the Hanover Exhibition in 1984 and 1991–95.

Sergio Asti

set up his own studio in 1953 and was one of the founding members of the ADI (Associazione per Il Disegno Industriale). He designs furniture, lighting, glassware, wooden products, ceramics, electrical appliances, interiors and exhibitions. He has received numerous awards including the gold medal at the XI Milan Triennale and a Compasso d'Oro (1962), and his work has been exhibited internationally.

Masayo Ave

was born in Tokyo in 1962 and graduated from the architectural department at Hosei University. After working in the architectural office of Ichiro Ebihara, she moved to Milan and completed her Master's degree in industrial design at the Domus Academy. She established her own design studio, Ave Design Co., in 1992. Since then she has received international acclaim for her work in industrial, furniture and textile design, theatre sets and architecture. She is particularly interested in the potential of new materials such as the Shibori textile, the fusion of traditional Japanese tie-dyeing techniques and modern technology.

Russell Barker

lives in High Wycombe, Buckingham where he runs his own lighting design company, Serious Design. He is currently producing designs for SKK, London.

Carlo Bartoli

was born in Milan where he graduated with a degree in Architecture from the Polytechnic. He is active in the fields of furniture and product design and has exhibited widely. The *Gaia* armchair is part of the permanent collection of the Museum of Modern Art in New York, and the *Sophia* chair can be seen in the collection of the Architectural Museum in Ljubljana. Bartoli teaches an Advanced Course of Industrial Design in Florence and Rome.

Leonor Bedel

graduated as a scenographer and interior designer and has practised architectural lighting design in Buenos Aires, Argentina since 1989. She is President of her own company which offers an architectural lighting service to architects and developers of corporate, commercial and institutional buildings throughout Argentina. Bedel is a member of the International Association of Lighting Designers and received an award at the 12th annual IALD awards in 1995. Notable lighting schemes include the Cesar Park Hotel, the renovation of the façade of the Puerto Madero pier and promenade, and the Rogelio Polesello exhibition at the Palais de Glace museum.

Franco Bettonica and Mario Melocchi

live and work in Milan. Bettonica graduated from the Faculty of Architecture in 1953, forming his own company, Frattini, which from 1954 collaborated with OPI (later to be known as Cini & Nils). His work can be seen in the permanent collection of the Museum of Modern Art, New York. Mario Melocchi was born in Parma in 1931 and founded OPI in 1956. Today he works in packaging and product design, designing collections for restaurants, offices and the home. He works with the architect Franco Bettonica, and their clients include Lancôme, L'Oreal, Nestlé and Philips.

Paolo Bistacchi and Lorenzo Stano

were born in Milan and Santeramo in 1947 and 1950, respectively. After artistic studies, Bistacchi became involved in industrial design, working with leading designers in Milan. He has been a member of ADI since 1984 and is also a member of BEDA. From 1978 to 1985 he worked as a lecturer at the Istituto Europeo di Disegno in Milan and also taught design in the industrial design department. He took part in the XVII Triennale in Milan and the 1995 Abitare il Tempo in Verona. He is currently a freelance designer working with clients such as Elam, Ycami Edizioni and Tre ci Luce. Lorenzo Stano graduated from the Istituto Europeo di Disegno in Milan. In 1971 he started a collaboration with Candle, becoming Art Director in 1987. He taught in the industrial design department of the Istituto Europeo but gave this up in 1987 to concentrate on his career as a designer. In 1994 he started a collaboration with Paolo Bistacchi.

Box Design & Products

was incorporated in 1988 and became independent in 1991. The directors, Russell Bagley and Hilary Heath, offer their own product range, custom-designed specials and complete lighting schemes. They also design and manufacture metal furniture and architectural metalwork. Notable projects include exterior lanterns for the Real World Studios, Wiltshire; feature chandeliers for the Grand Theatre Clapham, Battersea Arts Centre; custom design for Fitch used in Arthur Hayes Optometrists; spotlights for the Jigsaw retail outlets; a fluorescent uplighter for Alsop and Störmer's Hôtel du Département, Marseilles, and specialist lighting for Lord Rothschild's offices at Waddesdon Manor, Buckinghamshire.

John Bradley

formed his own multi-service consultant practice in 1972, specializing initially in mechanical and electrical engineering. John Bradley Associates have been appointed as consultants for many commercial and industrial developments and historically important structures in the UK and abroad. His appointment as consultant for the four-year restoration work at the Brighton Pavilion earned Bradley the Lighting Industry Federation 1995 Design Award for his floodlighting scheme for the exterior façades. Recently the practice has been commissioned by the Department of the Environment to produce street and flood-lighting proposals for the *Urban Design Guide for Whitehall*. They are also involved in advising on the exterior lighting of the Palace of Westminster.

Maurice Brill Lighting Design Ltd

is an architectural lighting design practice, founded in 1972 by Maurice Brill who had worked for several years in theatre lighting. As well as acting as light consultants, the company also designs special luminaires. Natural light plays an important role in most projects undertaken by the practice, and their services include daylight design. Maurice Brill Lighting Design is based in central London. Current projects include schemes for Windsor Castle; the Royal National Theatre, London; the Abjar Beach Hotel, Dubai; the Esprit retail chain, and the Hilton Hotel, Dead Sea, amongst others. Maurice Brill is also a founding partner of Light Directions Ltd in Hong Kong.

Sergio Calatroni

was born in San Guiletta, Italy in 1951 and studied at the Accademia di Belle Arti in Milan. He is currently involved in architecture, interior design and object design, sculpture and journalism. He is the founder of the design group Zeus, the Gallery Zeus Arte Milano in New York and the publishing company Editions Marrakech which specializes in books on design, architecture and art theory. His principal projects include offices in Osaka and Shizuoka; the Kashiyama boutique in Paris; the Fujitaka restaurant and the Seiren showroom in Milan, and the Copy Centre in Shizuoka. He has taught interior design at the Istituto Europeo di Disegno in Milan and product design at the Futurarium workshop in Ravenna. Calatroni is consultant editor of the design magazine *Interni* and has collaborated on design articles for most of the leading international design periodicals.

Enzo Catellani

is co-partner in the Italian lighting design company Catellani and Smith, which produces decorative lighting for domestic and commercial usage.

Marzio Rusconi Clerici and Laura Agnoletto

were born in Milan in 1960 and 1963, respectively. Clerici graduated from the Milan Polytechnic in 1987. Agnoletto attended the Classical Lyceum in Milan and is currently finishing a degree in philosophy. They have worked together for several years for companies such as Glas, Nemo and Fiorucci and are currently designing for Swatch. Other activities include design for television productions, interior design and architecture. They have participated in several exhibitions in Italy and abroad including the 'Light' show organized by Memphis (1988), the Alessandro Mendini exhibition 'Existens Maximum', Florence (1990), and 'La Fabbrica Estetica' at the Grand Palais, Paris (1993).

Lluis Clotet

was born in Barcelona in 1941 and studied at the Escuela Tecnica de Arquitectura in Barcelona, graduating in 1965. In 1964 he founded Studio PER with the architects Pep Bonet, Christian Cirici and Oscar Tusquets. He has collaborated in numerous projects with Tusquets. He is a founder member of Bd. Ediciones de Diseño, for which he still designs furniture and objects. He received the FAD award for the best interior in Barcelona in 1965 and 1972, and for the best building in 1978 and 1979. He has also received the Delta de Oro on three occasions for his industrial design. He exhibits widely both nationally and internationally.

Concord Sylvania

is the British subsidiary of SLI. The group has head offices in Geneva and manufacturing facilities in the UK, Belgium, Germany, France, Holland, Costa Rica and Australia. It comprises the following trade brands: Sylvania, Claude, Concord, Le Dauphin and Luminance. In the 1950s Concord Lighting, as it was then known, pioneered the concept and the production of architectural lighting. The company has worked with British design consultants such as Robert

Heritage who designed the classic *Power Flood* and was also responsible for the *Control Spots* range, launched in 1992. The Conran Design Group produced the award-winning *MIL* range and the 1991 *Quill* uplighter collection. Paul Atkinson designed *Torch*, *Talus* and in 1992 the *Hazul Duct*. Terence Woodgate set a new standard for low-voltage track lighting with the *Infinite System*, and Julian Powell-Tuck was responsible for the *Myriad* and *Optics* low-voltage ranges. In 1994 Concord's own design team was awarded the two most prestigious German lighting awards for its *LED 100* downlighter collection.

Nicholas Crosbie

was born in 1971 and studied at Central Saint Martin's College of Art and Design and at the Royal College of Art, London, receiving a Master of Arts degree in 1995. He founded Inflate and launched his first collection in 1995. At present he is working on a collection of furniture, an exhibition in Tokyo and various interior projects. His work has been featured in the leading European design magazines.

Rudolf Czapek

was born in 1965 in Vienna. He studied Fine Art in Vienna and New York. He established his own design studio in Vienna in 1991, and has since received awards for his work in Milan (1993) and Tokyo (1994).

Ross De Alessi Lighting Design

is a design company and consultancy based in Seattle which specializes in interior and exterior residential and commercial lighting. Ross De Alessi has worked in lighting design for over 22 years, completing over 700 major projects, and has received many lighting awards worldwide. He is a corporate member of the International Association of Lighting Designers and a member of the Illuminating Engineering Society. He frequently addresses retail, architectural, interior design and engineering conferences, and has taught at numerous colleges and universities.

Jean-Charles de Castelbajac

trained as a fashion designer and is now involved in interior, furniture and object design.

Michele de Lucchi

was born in Ferrara, Italy in 1951 and graduated from Florence University in 1975. During his student years he founded the 'Gruppo Cavat', a group concerned with avant-garde and conceptual architecture. He worked and designed for Alchimia until the establishment of Memphis in 1981. Today he produces exclusive art-orientated handmade products, industrial consumer items and furniture in wood, metal, stone and other materials for companies serving specialized markets. His architectural activities range from shop design to large-scale office buildings and private apartment blocks. De Lucchi's work has received many awards and he has published and exhibited widely both nationally and internationally. Due to his activities and vast experience in the most important period of Italian design, de Lucchi has been asked to teach at design schools and universities such as the Domus Academy, Milan and the University of Detroit.

Bernhard Dessecker

was born in 1961 in Munich. He studied interior architecture, then from 1983 to 1984 worked at Studio Morosa, New York. Since 1984 he has been a freelance designer, collaborating with the design team of Ingo Maurer.

Koen de Winter

was born in 1943 in Antwerp. He graduated in ceramic engineering from the Ecole des Métiers d'Art in Maredsoous before completing his education in industrial design at the Akademie Industriële Vormgeving in Eindhoven. After working for Volvo in Gothenburg, he returned to Holland and designed products for the Danish/Dutch housewares manufacturer Rosti-Mepal. Some of these designs are in the permanent collection of the Museum of Modern Art in New York. In 1979 he moved to Canada where he became vice president of design for Danesco Inc. For almost a decade he has been professor at the Université de Montréal and he is former president of the Association of Canadian Industrial Designers. Since 1990 his design office, Hippo Design, has developed products for a large number of Canadian and American companies. He has won several awards in industrial and graphic design, including the Design Canada Award.

David D'Imperio

was born in Allentown, Pennsylvania in 1960. He graduated from Kutztown University with a Bachelor of Fine Arts degree in graphic design in 1982. Today he designs and produces lighting, furniture and exhibition systems and has participated in numerous shows including the International Furniture Fair in Frankfurt. He currently lives and works in Miami.

The Ecart Group

was founded in 1978 by Andrée Putman. The practice is divided into three specific disciplines. Ecart SA is the design office, specializing in interior and product design ranging from hotels to shops, corporate offices to private houses, and museums to governmental offices. Notable designs include the Office of the Minister of Culture (1985); Ebel Headquarters (1985); Morgans Hotel, New York (1984); and the Im Wasserturm Hotel, Cologne (1989). Ecart International re-edits furniture and objects by such designers as Eileen Gray and Mariano Fortuny and edits designs by Ecart SA (designers include Patrick Naggar, Paul Mathieu and Michael Ray). Andrée Putman licensing division designs objects distributed throughout the world, including rugs, upholstery fabrics, tableware and bathroom accessories. Recent projects by Ecart SA are the Cartier Foundation exhibition areas (1993); the Sheraton Hotel, Paris-Roissy (1994); the Bally Boutiques concept (1993 to 1994), and the brand images of Baccarat and Swarovski.

Elliott & Associates Architects

provide services which include master planning, architectural, landscape and interior design, retail space design, image development, civil, structural, mechanical and electrical engineering, graphic design and signage, as well as product and lighting design. Projects range from retail, office, restaurant and residential through to municipal, city, state and federal government schemes, museum and historic restorations. They have been awarded over 80 major local, regional, national and international awards and their work has been published widely.

Hartmut Engel

was born in Stuttgart in 1939. He studied electrical engineering in Stuttgart and Darmstadt, then industrial design in Pforzheim. After qualifying as an industrial designer in 1968, he set up his own studio in Ludwigsburg. He has received numerous awards in Germany, including the Industrie Forum Design, Hanover Top Ten of the Year Gold Award.

Equation Lighting Design

was established in 1984 to provide architects and interior designers with a professional lighting design and consultancy service. They are active in the assessment of existing lighting installations, in the evaluation or development of performance criteria and the full design process.

Erco

was founded in 1934 in Lüdenscheid, Germany by Arnold Reininghaus, Paul Buschaus and Karl Reeber and specialized in the production of light fittings. By the 1960s Erco had gained the growing market for architectural lighting with tracks, spotlights and recessed downlights and today is a worldwide leader in the field, providing lighting schemes for diverse projects such as museums, display windows, universities, churches, discotheques, hotels, chain stores and administrative buildings and on occasion for private purposes.

Erco has received numerous awards, both national and international, for design, advertising and marketing.

Giancarlo Fassina

was born in Milan in 1935 and trained at the Superior Engineering Institute in Freiburg and the Milan Polytechnic where he graduated in architecture. In 1970 he joined Artemide, participating in the definition of all their products and working closely with Enzo Mari in the design of the *Aggregate System*. Recently he has collaborated with Marco Zanuso on the lighting of the new Fossati Theatre in Milan and with Mario Bellini on the lighting of the Milan Triennale's 'Home Design' show.

Oriano Favaretto

was born in 1956 in Treviso, Italy. He attended the Art School and the Academy of Fine Arts in Venice, and was awarded a grant from the Concorso tra Accademie d'Italia and the Lubiam prize in 1981. Other prizes include the Murano prize in 1987 in collaboration with Vetreria de Mahjo, and the Lampe d'Or prize at Sil in Paris (1993) in collaboration with Megalit.

André Feldmann and Arne Jacob Schultchen

were born in 1964 and 1965, respectively. They have worked as a team since they met at the Hochschule für Bildende Künste, Hamburg, from which they graduated in industrial design in 1992/93. In 1994 they established their own studio in Hamburg. Their work ranges from product, furniture, lighting and interior design to graphics, packaging, exhibition design and experimental works.

Maurizio Ferrari

was born in Monza, Italy in 1957 and received a degree in architecture from the Milan Polytechnic, followed by a Master's degree in Museography. He started his professional career in 1984, since which time he has collaborated with several lighting companies.

Fisher Marantz Renfro Stone

was founded over 20 years ago and now employs 16 designers. The practice offers services in general lighting design, equipment specification, daylight design and model studies, illumination calculations, budget development and energy-use analysis. Projects include the Bank of China, Hong Kong; the Sainsbury Wing, National Gallery, London; the National Gallery of Canada; Leo Burnett Corporate Headquarters, Chicago; the San Francisco Museum of Modern Art; the renovation of Carnegie Hall, New York, and the Rock and Roll Hall of Fame, Cleveland, Ohio.

Kazuko Fujie

established Studio F Atelier in 1977 and Fujie Kazuko Co. Ltd in 1987. In 1982 she created the object bench *Kujira* (Whale) constructed from panels of plywood. There followed the *Manjekyo* (Kaleidoscope) series in 1990, the *Morphe* series in 1992 and the *Mangekyo* series in 1994.

Gallegos Lighting Design

was founded in 1983 by Patrick Gallegos. It provides lighting designs for domestic and international projects which range in size from individual artist's works to major theme parks and entertainment complexes. Patrick Gallegos started his career in theatre lighting and has been designing light environments since 1973. He trained at the University of San Francisco, graduating with a Master of Fine Arts degree in lighting design from ECLA. He worked as a senior lighting designer for WED Enterprises (now Walt Disney Imagineering), where he designed and supervised the lighting of Walt Disney World's Epcot Centre. Current clients include Buena Vista Pictures Distribution, California Museum of Science and Industry, Walt Disney, Esherick Homsey Dodge and Davis Architects, Gensler and Associates, Hellmuth Obata and Kassabaum Architects, and Sony Theatres and Studios.

Jorge Garcia Garay

was born in Buenos Aires and licensed as an architect there, but has been working in design and the production of furniture and lighting in Barcelona since 1979. He has exhibited widely in Spain and also at the Design Museum, London in 1980 and 1990; the Museum für Angewandte Kunst in Cologne, 1992; the Design Centre, Essen and the University of Kansas, 1993. His most recent designs include the wall lights *Odeon* and *Roxy* and the *Solaris* lamp series.

Jose Martí Garcia

is an architect with a diploma from the Polytechnic in Valencia, Spain. Until 1986 he worked with various architectural studios including Vetges Tu and Mediterranea, whilst at the same time giving classes in decoration, and publishing numerous articles on industrial design. Since 1987 he has worked with Antonio Almerich.

Anna Gili

was born in Orvieto in 1960 and studied at the Istituto Superiore delle Industrie Artistiche, Florence, graduating in 1984 with a 'Sound Dress' project which has since been shown at the Padiglione di Arte Contemporanea in Milan, the Seibu Department Stores in Tokyo and the Kunstmuseum in Düsseldorf. She has designed objects for Alessi; tiles for Inax, Tokyo; ceramic pots for Richard Ginori; carpets, tapestries and furniture for Cassina; glass vases for Salviati and Bisazza; furniture and textiles for Cappellini, as well as furniture for Interflex and Playline. In 1992 she was the cultural co-ordinator of the exhibition 'Nuovo Bel Design' and in 1994 the curator of the exhibition and conference 'Primordi' which was held in the Triennale Building in Milan. Gili was also the curator of the exhibition 'Mutamenti' under the patronage of the Milan City Council (1995) and since 1990 has taught industrial design at the Accademia di Belle Arti in Milan.

Paolo Giordano

was born in Naples in 1954 and studied architecture in Milan. Today he lives and works in Milan and India as a designer and photographer, producing his own collection of furniture in limited edition in India.

Ernesto Gismondi

(who works also as Örni Halloween) was born in San Remo, Italy in 1931 and studied aeronautical engineering at the Milan Polytechnic and missile engineering at the School of Engineering in Rome. He taught in the machine institute of the Milan Polytechnic and was Associate Professor of Motors for Missiles. He co-founded Artemide in 1959 and, together with Sergio Mazza, developed new product lines drawing on his knowledge of specialist technologies. In 1981 he developed Memphis, a research laboratory for avant-garde design, and since 1989 has been involved with both Meta-Memphis and Memphis-Extra. He is Chairman of various companies in the Artemide Group. Other professional activities include being a member of the Board of Directors of EA The Triennal of Milan, and since 1994 a member of the Scientific Teaching Committee of the Higher Institute for Artistic/Industrial Design in Florence with appointment by the Ministry of Public Education. He is a Member of COSMIT, the organizing committee of the Milan Furniture Fair, and has headed and actively participated in numerous seminars in Italy and abroad on design and its developments, and on energy-saving applied to lighting.

Paolo Golinelli

was born in Milan in 1964 and graduated from the faculty of architecture, Milan University. After a collaboration with Studio Albini, he started working with Makio Hasuike on several industrial design projects. Clients include Vittorio Bonacina, De Vecchi, Ravarini Castoldi and Steel. Golinelli is assistant and researcher in the Faculty of Architecture, Milan University.

Tobias Grau

was born in Hamburg in 1957. He studied design in New York at the Parson's School of Design, after which he worked in the Design and Development office of Knoll International in Pennsylvania. He founded Tobias Grau KG in Hamburg in 1984, producing light designs for his own collection. Graudesign was set up four years later and under this name Grau redesigns hotels and showrooms and was responsible for the identity of 40 branches of the jeans shop Werdin. He also produces furniture and product designs. He has received awards in Germany and in 1993 received an *ID* magazine award, New York.

Johanna Grawunder

was born in 1961 in San Diego and received a Bachelor of Architecture degree in 1984 from the California State Polytechnic University, studying in Florence from 1983 to 1984. She is currently an architect with Sottsass Associati in Milan, where she has worked since 1985, becoming a partner in 1989. She has participated in several design exhibitions including 'Memphis Lights' (Milan, 1988); 'Women in Design' (Museum of Contemporary Design, Ravenna, 1990), and 'Chairs' (Milan, 1989), among others. In 1992 she presented a personal exhibition called 'Trucks' at Gallery Jannone (Milan) and Argentaurum Gallery (Belgium). She has designed objects for the Collection Cleto Munari, lamps for Salviati, a collection of objects for Giotto, Hong Kong, and marble pieces for Ultima Edizione.

Paul Gregory

was trained in theatrical lighting at the Goodman Theatre School of the Art Institute of Chicago and received a Master of Fine Arts degree in Architectural Lighting Design from the Parson's School of Design, New York. He was active in stage lighting for five years, working in regional theatres including the Alley Theatre, Stage West and the Goodman Theatre. He founded Litelab Corp. in 1975 and as its president was responsible for major design projects, including museums, restaurants and entertainment facilities. Gregory has received the Lumen IALD, Waterbury and *ASID* awards for his work. Recent lighting design projects include the Entel Tower in Santiago, Chile; the Dan Hotel in Eilat, Israel; the El Conquistador Hotel in Puerto Rico; the Knoll Headquarters in East Greenville, USA, and showrooms in Atlanta, Washington, Phoenix, Los Angeles, San Francisco and Toronto. Restaurant designs include the Planet Hollywoods in London, Chicago, Paris and 20 other cities.

Ashley Hall

was born in Cardiff, Wales in 1967. He studied furniture design at the University of Trent, Nottingham and the Royal College of Art, London, graduating in 1992. In 1994, after working as design co-ordinator at SKK Lighting, he founded his own practice and launched the *Homer* chair with Stephen Philips the following year. He has exhibited internationally and has continued to develop his skills on a range of products from lighting and furniture to small accessories for his own production and for other manufacturers.

Maria Christina Hamel

was born in New Delhi in 1958 but today lives and works in Milan. She began a collaboration with Alchimia in 1981 and later worked with Atelier Mendini. She is involved in domestic product design using ceramics, glass, silver and enamel, and also in the practice of applying chromatics to architectural structures. Since 1989 she has taken part in numerous exhibitions in Europe, holding solo shows in Milan and Verona. Hamel has taught at the University of Vienna, and the Art Schools of Faenza and Limoges. She was mentioned in the XVII Premio Compasso d'Oro for her saxophone design *Alessofono* which she created with Alessandro Mendini.

Marc Harrison

started his career as a builder and manufacturer of boats. He graduated from the Queensland College of Art in 1992, then established his own design and manufacturing business. He is currently mass producing four designs and continuing to produce one-off pieces of furniture.

Knud Holscher

was born in 1930 and studied at the School of Architecture, Royal Academy of Fine Arts, Copenhagen. He has been responsible for numerous award-winning large-scale public works in Norway, as well as smaller projects in France, Germany, Switzerland, Austria, Bahrain and the UK. Today he is a partner of Krohn and Hartvig Rasmussen Architects and Planners, with whom he has worked since 1968. From 1968 to 1988 he was Professor at the Royal Academy of Fine Arts, and in 1979 was made a member of the Danish Design Council. In 1990 he became design consultant for Erco Leuchten and in 1993 was awarded a prize from the Industrie Forum Design, Hanover for a range of lamps designed for Erco. He is a member of the Federation of Danish Architects, the Association of Academic Architects and the Council of Practising Architects and Industrial Designers, Denmark.

Isao Hosoe

was born in Tokyo in 1942. He received a Bachelor of Science degree in 1965 and a Master of Science degree (1967) in aerospace engineering from the Nihon University in Tokyo. He is currently a Professor of Design at the Domus Academy in Milan, at Milan Polytechnic and at the Istituto Superiore delle Industrie Artistiche, Florence, as well as at the University of Siena. He has received international acclaim for his design work including the Compasso d'Oro and a Gold Medal at the Milan Triennale. He has had one-man shows in Japan and the USA, and his work can be seen in the permanent collections of the Victoria and Albert Museum in London and the Centre Georges Pompidou in Paris.

Jordi Vilardell Iglesias

lives and works in Barcelona and is founder and director of the lighting design practice Gargot.

Malcolm Inglis

was born in Scotland in 1964. From 1981 to 1987 he studied architecture in Glasgow at the Mackintosh School of Architecture and was later awarded a scholarship to study art and architecture in Florence. From 1987 to 1988 he worked for Simister Monaghan McKinney Macdonald in Glasgow, then moved to Italy in 1988 where he collaborated extensively with King-Miranda Associati until 1995. Since 1995 he has been an associate with King Main & Ellison Architects in Glasgow and is also a part-time lecturer in product design at Glasgow School of Art.

Irideon

is a Dallas-based company founded in 1994 to provide lights with automated remote control functions for the architectural market. The parent companies Showco Inc. and Vari-Lite specialize in audio systems for the entertainment industry, and products for use in concerts, touring, theatre, corporate events and television applications, respectively.

Arne Jacobsen

(1902–71) studied at the Det Kongelige Danske Kunstakademi, Copenhagen under Kay Fisker. In 1927 he opened his own office in Hellerup. He was strongly influenced by the Modern architecture of the 1930s including that of Le Corbusier and Mies van der Rohe. His first major commission was the Bellavista housing project in Copenhagen. In 1950 Jacobsen started to design furnishings for mass production, notably for Fritz Hansen for whom he created the *Ant* and *Swan* chairs, the *Series 7* group and the *3107* office chair. Other clients included Allerød (furniture from 1932), Louis Poulsen (lighting), Stelton and Michelsen (silver and stainless steel), I.P. Lunds (bathroom fittings)

and C. Olesen (textiles). Architectural projects include St Catherine's College, Oxford (1964); the Danish National Bank, Copenhagen (1967), and the main administration building, Hamburgische Elektrizitäts-Werke, Hamburg (1970). Jacobsen received numerous awards worldwide, including, in the year of his death, the gold medal from the Académie d'Architecture de France.

Shiu-Kay Kan

is an architect who specializes in lighting design. Projects include a shopping centre in Malta, a nightclub in London and a conference centre in Beijing.

Wolfgang Karolinsky

studied musical composition at Vienna University, then opened an antique lighting shop in 1977. Today his company, Woka Lamps, has built up an international reputation for its faithful reproduction of classic designs by Hoffmann, Loos and the Wiener Werkstätte. He employs over 20 people producing highly crafted handmade pieces. In 1986 he organized a competition at the Academy of Applied Arts in Vienna, inviting students to produce lighting designs. The three winning designs were then put into production by Woka Lamps. At present Karolinsky is supervising a growing collection of contemporary lamps, each month selecting a design to produce. His work is exhibited internationally.

Masafumi Katsukawa

was born in Hyogo, Japan in 1960 and now lives and works in Milan. He graduated from the Kyoto Institute of Technology in 1983. In 1984 he moved to Italy and has collaborated with Studio Arosio, Studio Dada and Sottsass Associati. He is currently a freelance designer.

Perry A. King and Santiago Miranda

have been working together in Milan since 1976, operating in the fields of industrial, interior, interface and graphic design. In addition to working with some of the main

office furniture and lighting companies in Italy, King and Miranda have designed for manufacturers in the electromechanical and office equipment industries. Their interior design projects are to be found in Milan, Rome, Paris, London, Madrid and Tokyo, and they designed the exterior public lighting system for Expo '92 in Seville.

Laura Kohler

studied art and design then worked for a period as an interior designer. Today she has her own company, Loz Lampshades. Working for various designers, she supplies lampshades for commercial and domestic outlets throughout Britain.

Yasuo Kondo

was born in 1950 in Tokyo and graduated from the Interior Architecture Department of Tokyo University of Art and Design in 1973. Before founding his own design office in 1981 he worked both for Masahiro Miwa Environmental Design Office and Shiro Kuramata. To date projects have included restaurants, showrooms and domestic schemes in Japan, various national retail outlets and, in 1988, a boutique for Comme des Garçons Shirt (Paris and New York). He has won acclaim for his designs in Japan and the USA, being awarded the American Institute of Architects Design Prize in 1989. In the same year he published a book on his design philosophy entitled *Interior Space Designing*.

Defne Koz

was born in Ankara, Turkey in 1964 and is a freelance industrial and interior designer based in Istanbul and Milan. She studied in Ankara and Milan, receiving a Master's degree in Industrial Design from the Domus Academy. Clients include Steel, Foscarini, Alparda, Progetto-Oggetto, Pesaro and Ala Rossa. Koz has also undertaken domestic and retail interior design projects in Ankara. On first moving to Milan she spent two years at Sottsass Associati working on projects involving door handles, bathroom accessories, windows and solar cars.

Danny Lane

was born in Urbana, Illinois in 1955. Largely self-taught, he moved to England in 1975 to work with the stained-glass artist Patrick Reyntiens, then attended Central Saint Martin's College of Art and Design in London, studying painting with a strong emphasis on the esoteric tradition in art and design. In 1983 he co-founded Glassworks with John Creighton and began a three-year association with Ron Arad. He has extended his designs to include work with metal and wood, and has participated in numerous museum and gallery exhibitions and international furniture shows. In 1988 he held three one-man shows in Milan, London and Paris and started producing work for Fiam Italia. Since then he has participated in further individual shows and in 1990 received commissions for architectural artworks in Tokyo and Osaka. In 1994 he was commissioned by the Victoria and Albert Museum to install a balustrade of stacked glass in the Museum's new Glass Gallery and also held a one-man show at the Röhss Museum of Arts and Crafts in Göteborg, Sweden.

Louis A. Lara

was born in New York in 1964. He studied industrial design at the Pratt Institute in New York. Since 1986, through his own firm, he has designed a wide variety of products including lighting and furniture for both European and domestic clients and manufacturers. His work has been sold and published internationally and has been included in numerous gallery exhibitions across the USA.

Lighting Design Limited

was founded in 1981 by John Cullen who was later joined by Sally Storey. The company was originally called John Cullen Lighting Design but, following Cullen's death in 1986, split into two separate divisions: Lighting Design Limited which creates lighting solutions for the commercial sector, and John Cullen Lighting which specializes in domestic requirements. Sally Storey was appointed Chairman in 1986, and under her leadership the design team has won contracts in the UK, the USA, the Middle East and Europe. In 1995 the practice was awarded a commendation in the Lighting Design Awards for its work at the Peak Health Club in the Hyatt Carlton Tower Hotel, London.

Lighting Design Partnership

was founded in 1984 by Andre Tammes. Barry Hannaford became a partner in 1987, Douglas Brennan in 1990 and Graham Phoenix in 1995. With its head office in London and a small office in Edinburgh, the firm operates throughout the UK and has also worked in over 20 countries in Europe, Scandinavia, the Middle East, Australasia and North America. The directors' expertise lies in stage lighting, illuminating engineering and architecture. Projects undertaken include the lighting for Van Gogh's *The Irises*; the planning of the external lighting strategy for the city of Edinburgh; the lighting of 25 shopping centres and the largest Tibetan Buddhist temple outside Tibet. Clients include Euro Disney, Harrods, the Imperial War Museum, British Telecom, the Bank of England, the Royal Opera House, Sears and the Sheraton Management Corporation. LDP has received numerous awards, including citations from the International Association of Lighting Designers (1987, 1991); the Royal Institute of British Architects National Awards (1986, 1989 and 1991); and the National Lighting Award (1990).

Josep Lluscà

was born in Barcelona in 1948. He studied industrial design at the Escola Eina where he is now professor, and at the Ecole des Arts et Métiers, Montreal. He was Vice-president of ADI-FAD (Industrial Designers' Association) from 1985 to 1987, and was one of the founder members of the ADP (Association of Professional Designers). He is a member of the Design Council of the Catalonian government. He has been the recipient of several major awards, including the 1990 National Design Award and two prizes under 'ID Design Award in Furniture' presented by *ID* magazine, New York (1993, 1995). He frequently attends international exhibitions and conferences, most recently 'Catalonia 90's' in New York and 'International Design' at the Design Museum, London. Lluscà's work has been the subject of many publications, including a monograph (1991). Exhibitions have been held at various international design shows in Milan, Paris, Frankfurt, London, Tokyo, Nagoya, New York, Mexico City and Amsterdam.

Francesco Lucchese

was born near Messina, Italy in 1960. He graduated from Milan Polytechnic in 1985 and the same year was awarded the first prize in the competition 'Elemento di seduta per spazi collettivi' for his folding chair *Traslazione*. Also in 1985 he designed a glass chair sculpture for Busnelli which was exhibited at the Milan Furniture Fair. He has designed fabrics for Permaflex and decorative structures for the historical centre of Varese. Since 1986 he has been working in the lighting sector and co-operating with companies such as Egoluce, Quattrifolio, Candle, Contact and Luxo.

Marlin

is a British company formed in 1922 and trading initially under the name of Merchant Adventurers. In 1925 the company was taken over by the architects Boissevains and by 1932 started to work in lighting when it was awarded the contract for lighting the Royal Corinthian Yacht Club, followed shortly by Shellmax House on the Embankment, London. The name Marlin was adopted in 1973, by which time the company employed over 400 people. In 1985 it was acquired by Emess plc, a company which focuses on consumer and commercial lighting with subsidiaries such as JSB, Eclatec in France and Brilliant in Germany.

Ingo Maurer

was born in 1932 on the Island of Reichenau, Lake Constance, Germany and trained in typography and graphic design. In 1960 he emigrated to the USA, working as a freelance designer in New York and San Francisco before returning to Europe in 1963. He founded Design M in Munich in 1966, and since then his lighting designs have achieved worldwide recognition. He has exhibited widely, including 'Ingo Maurer: Making Light' at the Museum Villa Stuck, Munich and 'Licht Licht' at the Stedelijk Museum in Amsterdam, and his work forms part of the permanent collections of many museums, including the Museum of Modern Art, New York.

Mark McDonnell

was born in Cairo in 1954 but today lives and works in Marin County, California. He was educated at the Rhode Island School of Design where he received a Bachelor of Fine Art degree in sculpture in 1979. From 1987 to 1991 he was Chairman of the Glass Department at the California College of Arts and Crafts in Oakland. His work can be seen in the permanent collections of numerous design museums including the Musée des Arts Décoratifs, Paris; the Corning Museum of Glass, New York, and the Cooper-Hewitt Museum of the Smithsonian Institution, New York.

Richard Meier

was born in Newark, New Jersey in 1934. He studied architecture at Cornell University, after which he worked for architects Davis, Brody and Wisniewski in New York, followed by Skidmore, Owings and Merrill and Marcel Breuer. In the late 1950s and early 1960s he worked as an artist with Michael Graves but set up his own architectural practice in New York in 1963. He has been Professor of Architecture at Harvard and Yale Universities as well as at the Cooper Union, and in the 1970s was a member of the New York Five with Peter Eisenman, Michael Graves, Charles Gwathmey and John Hejduk who advocated

a Modernist ideal strongly reminiscent of Le Corbusier's Cubist designs of the 1920s. Much of Meier's work at this time was derivative of previous 20th-century designs, for example a tea set for Alessi in the style of Malevich and Hoffmanesque metalwork and ceramics for Swid Powell. Architectural work includes the Museum for Kunsthandwerk, Frankfurt (1984); the High Museum, Atlanta (1984); the Getty Museum in Los Angeles (1985) and the City Hall in The Hague (1985). Richard Meier's work has been the subject of many solo exhibitions worldwide and he has been the recipient of accolades such as the Arnold W. Brunner Memorial Prize, the Reynolds Memorial Award and the Pritzker Architecture Prize. His life story has been the subject of a monograph and a television film.

Friedbert Meinert

was born in 1953 in Germany. He trained as an engineering patternmaker in Stuttgart and moved to London in 1974. He studied product design at Middlesex Polytechnic and also has a postgraduate teaching diploma. He was Managing Director of Aktiva Systems from 1988 to 1991 where he designed and developed low-voltage lighting systems. He is now Managing Director of Basis Design which specializes in lighting design manufacture and light planning. Recent projects include specialist library lighting for St John's College, Cambridge, designed by Edward Cullinan Architects, display lighting for Ford Motor Company by Imagination and retail lighting for Harrods, London.

Alessandro Mendini

was born in Milan in 1931. For many years he has been the theorist of avant-garde design, co-founding the Global Tools Group in 1973 as a counter-movement to established Italian design. In 1978 he started his collaboration with Studio Alchimia in Milan and developed the so-called 'Banal Design' which sought to change items in daily use into new and

ironical objects. In 1983 he became Professor of Design at the University of Applied Art in Vienna, and from 1983 to 1988 collaborated with designers such as Achille Castiglioni, Riccardo Dalisi and Aldo Rossi in Casa dell Felicità for Alessi. An architect, furniture and product designer, he is Art Director of Swatch Lab of Milan and of Alessi. He has been Editor of the magazines *Casabella*, *Modo* and *Domus*, and his many awards include the Compasso d'Oro, an honour from the Architectural League of New York and the distinction of Chevalier des Arts et des Lettres. In 1990 he set up Atelier Mendini with his brother, architect Francesco Mendini, designing projects such as the Groninger Museum in Holland and – with Yumiko Kobayashi – the Paradise Tower, Hiroshima.

Alfonso Milà

was born in 1924 and studied architecture in Barcelona, graduating in 1952. He then collaborated in an architectural practice with Federico Correa. He was a member of the Board of Architects Association of Catalonia and, from 1970, Professor at the School of Architecture in Barcelona. Buildings by Correa and Milà include the Godó y Trias factory in Barcelona (1962). Milà has received numerous design awards in Spain and in 1986 his work was included in the exhibition 'Contemporary Spanish Architecture: An Eclectic Panorama' held at the Architectural League in New York.

Miguel Milà

was born in 1931 and studied interior design at the School of Architecture, Barcelona. After graduating, he worked with his brother Alfonso Milà and with Federico Correa. His clients include B.d. Ediciones de Diseño, Santa & Cole and Polinax. He received the 1965 ADI-FAD award and the 1987 National Design Prize.

Inao Miura

was born in Tokyo in 1942. He has a Bachelor of Arts degree from the Musashino University of Art in Tokyo. In 1969 he moved to Italy where he has collaborated with Sergio Asti's design studio in Milan.

Torsten Neeland

was born in 1963 in Hamburg and graduated in industrial design from the Hochschule für Bildende Künste. Work for his own practice includes interior design projects such as the Uta Raasch fashion stores, Düsseldorf (1988) and Hamburg (1991–2); a doctor's office in Hamburg (1993) and the Go shoe shop (1993). He is equally well known for his product design, producing a range of items including candlesticks, lamps and bowls for Anta; a coat hanger for Anthologie Quartett; furniture for Reim Interline and a cosmetic counter for Estée Lauder. He has exhibited his work in Europe and has had a joint show at the Düsseldorf Museum of Arts.

Marc Newson

was born in Sydney in 1963 and graduated from the Sydney College of Art in 1984. In 1985 the Powerhouse Museum in Sydney acquired some of his designs for their permanent collection, at the same time offering him a Craft Council Grant to devise new work. Since 1987 he has worked periodically in Japan for Idée, creating, amongst other designs the *Rattan* and *Felt* series. Newson lives and works in Paris and is currently working on new designs and forthcoming exhibitions in New York and Los Angeles.

Novell/Puig Design

was founded in 1991 by the industrial designers Josep Novell and Josep Puig. Novell was born in 1953. Since 1984 he has been Professor of Industrial Design at the Elisava school, Barcelona. Puig was born in 1959. He became Professor of Industrial Design at Elisava in 1982 and is also a professor at the EINA school. He was a founder member of the experimental design group Transatlantic (1984–9). The company has received numerous awards in Spain.

Luciano Pagani and Angelo Perversi

were both born in Milan in 1950 and graduated in architecture from Milan Polytechnic. Before setting up their design studio they worked individually in the fields of architecture and lighting design for companies such as Flos, Mondadori and Rizzoli, and collaborated with both the Architecture Faculty of Milan University and with the Domus Academy. They have received international acclaim for their work, being awarded the Compasso d'Oro in 1987 and the Product Design Award IBD in 1992. Pagani and Perversi started their collaboration with Zanotta in 1993.

Roberto Pamio

has worked near Venice since graduating in architecture from Venice University in 1968. His projects include both domestic and industrial design for clients such as Cadel, Matteograssi and Leucos. He has worked in the USA, Australia, Mexico and Japan as well as in Italy, and has received international recognition for his work including four Roscoe awards. Today he has two studios, one in Scorze, Venice and the second in New York.

Jorge Pensi

is a Spanish architect and industrial designer, born in 1946 in Buenos Aires. He has worked in Barcelona since 1977, specializing in the design of furniture, lighting, fittings and product image. He has been associated with Perobell, the SIDI group, Amat, B.Lux and the magazine *On Diseño*. Pensi has achieved wide acclaim for his designs, most notably the *Toledo* chair for which he was given the first Award Selection SIDI-1988, two silver Deltas and an Award Design-Auswahl 90 from the Stuttgart Design Centre. Since 1989 he has worked with companies in Italy, Germany, Finland and the USA in the area of product design. In recent years, as well as his professional work, he has started to give courses and conferences in various countries.

Maurizio Peregalli

was born in Varese, Italy in 1951. He is responsible for the design of the Armani shops and showrooms in Milan and in 1984 completed his first furniture collection for his own design studio, Zeus. He is also a partner in Noto which produces the Zeus collections.

Dominique Perrault

was born in Clermont-Ferrand, France in 1953 and studied architecture at the Ecole des Beaux-Arts, Paris. He gained a certificate of advanced studies in town planning from the National School of Bridges and Roadways, Paris, as well as a Master's degree in History from the School of Advanced Studies in Social Sciences. Before opening his own studio in 1981 he worked for Martin van Treck, René Dottelonde and Antoine Grumbach. In 1983 Perrault was the winner of the 'Programme for New Architecture' (PAN XII), France and the 'Album of Young Architecture', Ministry of Housing, France, and in 1986 was made consultant architect for the Loiret District Council. Today he is also the consultant architect for the city of Nântes and is on the Council for Urban Planning in the city of Salzburg. Perrault has been a member of the board of the French Institute of Architecture and of the Scientific and Technical Committee, ESA, in Paris since 1988. He has been the recipient of numerous awards, including second prize for town planning from the Foundation of the Academy of Architecture for his Bibliothèque de France project. In 1993 he was awarded the Grand Prix National d'Architecture.

Andrée Putman

was born in Paris and studied music at the Paris Conservatoire with François Pulenc before becoming a stylist and journalist. In 1971 she founded the design company

Créateurs et Industriels, working with fashion designers such as Issey Miyake and Jean-Charles de Castelbajac. Today, her own enterprise, Ecart International, focuses on the production and revival of classic furniture design and modernist accessories. She has worked with deSede, Charles Jourdan, Sasaki and Toulemonde Bochart among other companies, and her interior design projects have brought her world fame. These include the Morgans Hotel, New York; the Wasserturm Hotel, Cologne; Le Lac, Japan; villas and shops for the clock and watch company Ebel; offices for the French Minister of Culture; an art museum in Rouen, and the Museum of Modern Art in Bordeaux. Work carried out in 1993/1994 includes the headquarters of Air France; the Sheraton Hotel, Paris-Roissy and the concept for the chain of Bally shoe shops worldwide.

Michael Ramharter

was born in Vienna in 1961. He studied as a gold- and silversmith before enrolling at the Academy of Applied Arts in Vienna where he studied product design. In 1988 he founded his own studio and the following year joined the group 31st May. He was awarded a scholarship from the Ministry of Education and Arts in 1992, since which time he has held numerous exhibitions in Vienna, Brussels, Bern, Paris, Berlin and Hanau. His work can be seen in the permanent collection of the Museum of Applied Arts in Vienna.

Karim Rashid

was born in Cairo in 1960. In 1982 he received a Bachelor of Industrial Design degree from Carleton University in Ottawa, Canada. He completed his graduate studies in Italy under Ettore Sottsass and Gaetano Pesce, then moved to Milan for a one-year scholarship at the studio of Rodolfo Bonetto. On his return to Canada he worked for seven years with KAN Industrial Designers in Toronto as head designer on projects ranging from high-tech products to furniture. He also co-founded and designed

the Babel Collection (a clothing range for men and women), before setting up North Studio, a conceptual-based studio producing objects for exhibitions and galleries worldwide. Since 1991 he has been principal designer for Karim Rashid Industrial Design. Projects include furniture, lighting, houseware and product designs. Rashid has been a faculty member at the Ontario College of Art and a full-time assistant professor at the Rhode Island School of Design. Today he is Assistant Professor of Industrial Design at the Pratt Institute, New York and at the University of the Arts, Philadelphia. He has received many design awards, most recently the Good Design Award for Permanent Collection 1995 from the Chicago Museum of Design.

Sarah Reilly

trained in London as a sculptor and a ceramicist. She designs one-off pieces, limited editions and site-specific projects and works mainly with interior designers and architects. Her work has been published in leading European design magazines.

Massimo Sacconi

is an architect and is also the designer of technical products for Osram, Targetti and Siemens.

Marc Sadler

graduated in industrial design in Paris, after which he carried out extensive research in the use of new plastic materials, specializing in the design of sports equipment and accessories. After an extended trip to the Far East he moved to the USA and opened a studio in New York. At the same time he created a workshop in Asolo staffed with a team of model-makers and technicians where he developed a new multi-use product, *Totem*, and began his collaboration with Far Eastern manufacturers. His clients include Cartier, Danese, Ebel Suisse, Fiorucci, Reebok and Intersport Swiss.

Masatoshi Sakaegi

was born in 1944 in Chiba-ken, Japan. In 1983 he founded the Masatoshi Sakaegi Design Studio which specializes in ceramic and melamine tableware and ceramic sculpture. He has won many awards for his work, most recently at the 4th International Ceramics Competition '95, Mino, Japan. In 1991 he became an assistant professor at the Art University of the Province of Aichi.

Denis Santachiara

was born in Reggio-Emilia, Italy and now lives and works in Milan. He collaborates with major European manufacturers such as Oceano Oltreluce, Artemide, Kartell, Vitra, Yamagiwa, Domodinamica and Zerodisegno. His work has been exhibited in private and public galleries, and he has taken part in the Venice Biennale and Documenta Kassel, as well as the Milan Triennale in 1982, 1985, 1986 and 1988.

Schuler & Shook Inc.

was founded in 1986 by Duane Schuler and Robert Shook, both of whom had been practising architectural lighting design for several years. The partners have a strong background in theatrical lighting design, working in theatres and opera houses all over the world. With offices in Chicago and Minneapolis, Schuler and Shook cover a wide scope of services and a range of project types including retail spaces, restaurants, offices, churches, museums, zoos, building exteriors, site lighting and special events. Schuler and Shook have received numerous design prizes such as awards from the International Association of Lighting Designers and the General Electric Company.

Zeukyau Shichida

was born in Yokohama, Japan in 1964. He studied architecture at the Musashino University of Art, graduating in 1988, then worked as an editor on the design magazine *Icon*. Since 1991 he has been a freelance editor and has worked for various design and architecture periodicals. In

1994 Shichida established his own brand name, Kwau Shau An, designing and manufacturing lighting, furniture and accessories for the home and office.

Ettore Sottsass

was born in 1917 in Innsbruck and is one of the most important designers of this century. He completed his architectural studies in 1939 at the University of Turin and since 1947 has been working as a designer in Milan. In 1958 he became the chief consultant for design at Olivetti and was responsible for a number of innovative design concepts in information electronics. During this period of consultancy Sottsass became involved in experimental projects, starting with the radical architecture of the 1960s. This work was followed up with the Memphis Group, which initiated the New Design of the 1980s. Sottsass Associati was founded in 1980. Sottsass's clients include major manufacturers such as Alessi, Cassina, Mitsubishi, Olivetti, Seiko, Zanotta, Esprit and Knoll. Among his recent architectural projects are interior furnishings for Esprit; the 'Zibibbo' bar in Il Palazzo Hotel, Fukuoka, Japan; the Daniel Wolf apartment block in Colorado; and a hotel and shopping mall in Kuala Lumpur. His work has been exhibited in numerous galleries and museums worldwide.

Ayala Sperling-Serfaty

was born in Israel in 1962. Following early education and military service in Israel, she studied Fine Art at Middlesex Polytechnic, UK and art history and philosophy at Tel Aviv University. She was awarded a scholarship from the Sharet Fund, Israel, in 1984 and presented with first prize in the Annual Furniture Design Competition in Israel in 1993. Her work has been exhibited nationally and has been published in Israel, Japan and Italy.

Philippe Starck

was born in Paris in 1949. After a period of activity in New York, he returned to France where he has since built up an international reputation. He has been responsible for major interior design schemes, including the late François Mitterrand's apartment at the Elysée Palace, the Café Costes, and the Royalton and Paramount hotels in New York. He has also created domestic and public multi-purpose buildings such as the headquarters of Asahi Beer in Tokyo. As a product designer he works for companies throughout the world, collaborating with Alessi, Baleri, Baum, Disform, Driade, Flos, Kartell, Rapsel, Up & Up, Vitra and Vuitton. His many awards include the Grand Prix National de la Création Industrielle. His work can be seen in the permanent collections of all the major design museums.

Stiletto

is the pseudonym of Frank Schreiner, born in 1959 in Berlin. He studied visual communication at the Hochschule der Künste, Berlin, then graphics at the Kunstakademie, Düsseldorf. He has exhibited his work in Germany, Austria and the USA. Since 1981 he has been involved in experimental graphics, television, art and object design, setting up Stiletto Studios in 1991.

Targetti Sankey

is a leading Italian manufacturer of lighting products. It was established in 1928 as a craftsman's workshop but became renowned in the 1950s for its innovative and versatile domestic lighting designs. The commercial lighting sector was developed in the 1970s with the production of electrified tracks, spotlights and downlights attaining international recognition with the *Structura System*. The latest aspect of the company's development is the creation of a Research Centre of Technical Lighting and Photometric Measurements in co-operation with the Engineering Department of Florence University. Targetti has nine branches (Italy, France, Germany, the UK, Spain, Holland, Sweden, Hong Kong, New Zealand) and three production branches (Spain, Brazil, the Philippines). Recently the Italian division has diversified into the lighting of works of art and historical sites and has been chosen to light Notre Dame Cathedral in Paris and Michelangelo's *David* in Florence.

Matteo Thun

was born in Bolzano, Italy in 1952. He attended the Oskar Kokoschka Academy in Salzburg and graduated in architecture from the University of Florence. He was a partner in Sottsass Associati and a member of the Memphis Group from 1979 to 1984. At present he is involved mainly with industrial design, architecture, furnishings and corporate product design, graphics and packaging. He exhibits and lectures widely, and his work has won numerous awards. His designs appear in the permanent collections of many leading art and design museums, including the Cooper-Hewitt Museum, New York and the Victoria and Albert Museum, London.

Renato Toso and Noti Massari

are lighting designers now working with Leucos in Venice. They both graduated from Venice University in 1967 and have worked for glass, lighting, ceramic and furniture manufacturers.

Katrien Van Liefferinge

originally trained as a cabinet-maker in Belgium, her native country. She completed her studies in Britain at Leeds Metropolitan University and Glasgow School of Art, gaining a Bachelor of Art degree in Three-dimensional Design and a Master of Art degree in Art and Design. From one-off commissions to product and theatre design, her work has received critical acclaim in Paris and New York.

Frans Van Nieuwenborg and Martijn Wegman

established themselves as industrial designers in 1982 in Leiden. The firm is involved in the product development of small, medium and multi-national companies for the national and international market.

Villiers Brothers

was established by Harry, Tim and Hugo Villiers in 1989 and produces furniture and lighting. Harry Villiers has a degree in graphic design and worked as an art director in advertising and then as a set designer in the film and television industry in Australia and America. Tim Villiers completed an indentured welding apprenticeship and worked in the North African oil-fields before starting his own architectural steelwork and engineering company. Hugo Villiers completed a City and Guilds motorcycle engineering and design course and worked with the Cambridge Arts Theatre prior to setting up his own set construction and props.-making company. The brothers have exhibited their work at the Worshipful Company of Blacksmiths' show at the Barbican (1992); at Euroluce, Milan, and at Decorex 1994.

Hans von Klier

was born in Tetschen, Czechoslovakia in 1934 and graduated in industrial design from the Hochschule für Gestaltung, Ulm in 1959. He collaborated with Ettore Sottsass on numerous projects for Olivetti while working in his Milan office from 1960 to 1968. Since 1969 he has been in charge of the Olivetti Corporate Identity Department. He has sat on the jury panel of a number of national and international design awards and took part in the Milan Triennale in 1973 and 1975.

Rätus Wetter

was born in Appenzell, Switzerland, and initially trained as a florist. In 1989 he attended the Academy of Applied Arts in Vienna studying industrial design. His work has been exhibited in Germany, Austria and Spain.

Hannes Wettstein

was born in Ascona, Switzerland in 1958. He is involved in furniture, lighting, product and interior design and architecture. He has worked with Baleri Italia since 1985 and with other manufacturers such as Revox, Kleis, Belux, Ventura, Oluce Italia, Philips and Ritzenhoff. Today he is a partner in 9-D Design, Zurich, which he co-founded in 1993.

Weyers & Borms

were born in the 1960s and are self-taught designers.

Hans Wolff & Partners

is an independent Dutch company, principally concerned with theatre consultancy, architectural lighting, and theatre and television lighting design. Recently the practice has produced designs for offices, shops, theatres, museums and trade shows, and it is currently working on a shopping mall, the head office of a bank, two museums, a chapel, a pilot store for the largest supermarket chain in The Netherlands, and exterior landscaping projects.

Leonid Yentus

was born in Odessa, USSR in 1945 and attended the Moscow Stroganoff Industrial Art School in 1974. In 1989 he emigrated to New York where he joined the Atelier of Gaetano Pesce. An exhibition, interior and furniture designer, he founded his own company, Y Design, in New York in 1995. He has participated in several group shows in the USA and Canada, and his works have been published in Italy and the USA. In 1990 he took part in project research for '100% Make-Up' for Officina Alessi. A number of his furniture pieces are in the Rutgers University Art Museum, New Jersey and the Montreal Museum of Decorative Arts, Quebec.

Project Credits

page 116

Peak Health Club, Hyatt Carlton, London, UK

Client
The Hyatt Carlton Tower Hotel

Lighting design
Sally Storey, Chris Lewis

Suppliers
Chelsom Ltd, Genesis, Hitech Lighting, Erco, Light Projects, Concord, RS Robertson

Contractor
Balfour Kilpatrick

page 118

SPoT Bagel Bakery, Seattle, Washington, USA

Client
Jay Glass, President SPoT Bagel Bakery

Architect and lighting designer
Adams/Mohler Architects

Suppliers
Lightolier (recessed compact fluorescent downlights and track lighting), Lava Simplex International (lava lamps)

Contractor
Krekow Jennings Inc

page 120

De Vere Grand Harbour Hotel, Southampton, UK

Client
De Vere Hotels

Architect
Igal Yawetz & Associates Ltd

Lighting design
Maurice Brill Lighting Ltd

Interior design
Ezra Attia Associates International

Suppliers
Lucent Lighting Ltd, Genesis Lighting Ltd, Designed Architectural Lighting Ltd, McCloud & Co., Outdoor Lighting Supplies, Concord Lighting, Oldham Lighting Ltd, Erco Lighting Ltd, Futimis Ltd, White Light Ltd, Light Projects Ltd, Chelsom Ltd, Siemens Ltd, R & S Robinson, Montrose International, Lightscape Projects Ltd, Commerical Lighting Systems Ltd, B.B.I. Ltd, iGuzzini Ltd, Hoffmeister, GFC Lighting Ltd, Marlin Lighting

page 148

Mexican Gallery of the British Museum, London, UK

Client
Consejo Nacional para la Cultura y las Artes/Instituto Nacional de Antropologia e Historia di Mexico

Architect
Teodoro González de Léon

Lighting design
Fisher Marantz Renfro Stone

Suppliers
Designed Architectural Lighting (D.A.L.), Erco Lighting

page 150

Reading Rooms of the Biblioteca de Catalunya, Barcelona, Spain

Client
Department of Culture, Generalitat de Catalunya

Architect
Joan Rodon

Lighting design
Erco Leuchten GmbH

page 152

Belgo Centraal Restaurant, Covent Garden, London, UK

Client
Belgo Centraal

Architect
Ron Arad, Alison Brooks

Lighting design
Ron Arad Associates

Collaborating designer
Basis Design Ltd

Contractor
Delcon Construction Ltd

Electrical contractor
Jets Electrical Ltd

page 154

National Museum of Natural History, Paris, France

Architect
Jules André

Restoration
Paul Chemetov, Borja Huidobro

Lighting design
Erco Leuchten GmbH (industrial), René Allio (light settings)

page 156

Birmingham School of Art, Birmingham, UK

Client
Birmingham School of Art

Architect
Associated Architects

Lighting design
Concord Sylvania Specials Department

Contractor
N. G. Bailey

page 158

Basilica Nuestra Señora del Pilar, Buenos Aires, Argentina

Client
Basilica del Pilar

Architect
Pombo & Lamarca

Lighting design
Leonor Bedel & Asociados

Suppliers
Reggiani (lighting fixtures), Osram (lighting sources)

Electrical contractor
Eger srl

page 160

Bibliothèque Nationale de France, Paris, France

Client
Ministry of Culture, Department for Public Buildings, Institute of the Bibliothèque Nationale de France

Architect
Dominique Perrault

Lighting design
Gaëlle Lauriot Prévost, Inge Waes

Contracting authority consultants
Jean-Paul Lamoureux (lighting and acoustics)

BET
Technip Seri Construction

Suppliers
Sammode (suspended fittings, fluorescent tube, security lighting in public areas, spots, spots on horizontal poles), Wila (recessed downlighters in public areas, indirect lighting on masts in lighting rooms, lighting on horizontal poles, inset pavement and wall lights), Seae (lighting sheets), Marlin (recessed downlighters in the tower offices and lobbies), Zumtobel (fluorescent tubes with screens in parking area, fluorescent tubes in the underground stockrooms of the towers), Thorn Europhan (built-in markings on the floor), Mazda and Petitjean (lighting masts on the esplanade), Erco (spots on beams in the conference rooms), Meyer (downlighters in the garden), Wibre (security lighting in the garden)

page 162

Manchester Airport Pedestrian Walkway/Fixed Link, Manchester, UK

Client
Manchester Airport plc

Architect
Aukett Associates

Lighting design
Lighting Design Partnership

Suppliers
Zumtobel, Artemide, Marlin, Meyer (luminaires), GE Lighting, Oldham Lighting (lamps)

Electrical contractor
Travers Morgan

page 164

Santa Barbara County Courthouse, Santa Barbara, California, USA

Client
BEGA US

Architect
William Mooser III

Lighting design
Ross De Alessi Lighting Design

Supplier
BEGA (floodlights)

Electrical contractor
Del May Electric

Suppliers

Adams/Mohler Architects
3515 Fremont Avenue N., Seattle,
Washington 98103, USA

Afro City Edition
Corso Porta Nuova 46/B, Milan 20121, Italy

Antonio Almerich SL
41 Ciudad de Liria, Paterna 46980,
Valenica, Spain

ANTworks
81 Vale Street, Moorooka 4105, Queensland,
New South Wales, Australia

Amedei Tre snc
Amedei 3, Milan 20123, Italy

Antonangeli Illuminazione srl
Via E. de Amicis 42, Cinisello Balsamo 20092,
Milan, Italy

OUTLETS
Benelux
Danver Light, 63 Tabaksvest, 2000 Antwerp,
Belgium

Canada
Artemide Canada Ltd, 9200 Place Picasso,
Montreal, St Leonard, Quebec H1P 3JB

France
C & D Diffusion, 23 Rue de Savoie, 75700
Sallanches

Germany
Salvo Causarano, 2 Katharinenstrasse,
59348 Ludinghausen

Spain
Dimmer scv, 61–20A c/Jesus, 46007 Valencia

Ron Arad Studio
62 Chalk Farm Road, London NW1 8AN, UK

Arteluce, Division of Gruppo Flos SpA
Via Angelo Faini 2, Bovezzo, Brescia 25073,
Italy

OUTLETS
Belgium
Flos SA, Gossetlaan 50, 1720 Groot-Bijgaarden

France
France Flos sarl, 5 rue de Bicêtre, 94240
L'Hay Les Roses

Germany
Deutschland Flos GmbH, Am Probsthof 94,
53121 Bonn

Japan
Flos Co. Ltd, PMC Building, 1-23-5 Higahi-
Azabu, Minato-ku, Tokyo 106

Spain
Flos SA, c/Bovedillas 16, San Just Desvern,
08960 Barcelona

Switzerland
Flos SA, 75 Blvd St-Georges, 1025 Geneva

UK
Flos Ltd, 31 Lisson Grove, London NW1 6UB

USA
Flos Inc., 200 McKay Road, Huntington
Station, New York, NY 11746

Artemide SpA
Via Bergamo 18, Pregnana Milanese 20010,
Milan, Italy

OUTLETS
Australia
Ornare, 14 Ormond Avenue, 5072 Magil

Austria
Vertreter Design Agentur R. Greinecker,
Herbeckstrasse 27, 1183 Vienna

Belgium/The Netherlands/Luxembourg
Horas SA, Beemstraat 25, 1601 Ruisbroek

Canada
Artemide Canada Ltd, 9200 Place Picasso,
Montreal, St Leonard, Quebec H1P 3JB

Cyprus
HC Furniture and Art Ltd, 24 Pindarou Str.,
PO Box 586, Nicosia

Denmark/Finland/Sweden/Norway
Renzo d'Este, H.E. Teglersvej 5, 2920
Charlottenlund

France
Artemide E.u.r.l., 6–8 rue Basfroi, 75011 Paris

Germany
Artemide GmbH, Ltterpark 5, D-4010 Hilden

Greece
Habitat – K. Frampton & Co. 9 Herodotou
Street, Athens 10674

Hong Kong
Artemide Ltd, 102–103 Ruttonjiee Centre,
Duddel Street

Japan
Artemide Inc., 4-5-18 Higashi Nippori,
Arakawa-ku, Tokyo 106

Korea
Kunyang Trading, Kangnam-Gu, Yeoksam-
Dong 721-39, PO Box 7594, Seoul 135-080

New Zealand
ECC Lighting Ltd, 39 Nugent Street,
PO Box 291, Auckland

Portugal
FNI - Fabbrica Nacional de Iluminaçao SA,
Avenida Leite De Vasconcelos, Lote 16,
Apartado 3, Alfragide, 2700 Amadora

Singapore
Concept Lighting Pte Ltd, 356 Alexandra
Road, 0315 Singapore

Spain
Artemide SA, C/Ripolles 5 y 7, 08820 Prat de
Llobregat, Barcelona

Switzerland
Artemide Illuminazione AG, Via Trevano 72,
6900 Lugano

Turkey
Fil Mimari AS, Spor-Cad, 159 Akaretier,
80680 Istanbul

UK
Artemide GB Ltd, 323 City Road,
London EC1V 1LJ

USA
Artemide Inc., National Sales and Customer
Service Center, 1980 New Highway,
Farmingdale, NY 11735

Ave Design Corporation
10-5-311 Ishikawa-cho, 2-chome-Ota-ku,
Tokyo 145, Japan

Axis Lighting Inc.
6300 ave du Parc No. 316, Montreal,
Quebec H2V 4H8, Canada

Baldinger Architectural Lighting
19–02 Steinway Street, Astoria,
NY 11105, New York, USA

OUTLETS
Canada
R.D. Sales, 104–120 Fort Street,
Winnipeg, Manitoba R3C 1C7

Germany/Austria/Switzerland
Brendel Leuchten GmbH & Co. KG, BE28
Mecklenburgische Strasse, Berlin, Germany

Japan
Yamagiwa Ltg. Ctr, 4F, 4-5-18 Higashi-
Nippori, Arakawa-ku, Tokyo 116

Mexico
Comercializadora de Industrias, Piramid
Moctezuma 110-2 Sur Col. Del Valle,
Garza Garcia, Nuevo Leon 66220

Basis Design Limited
Units 17–18, 109 Bartholomew Road,
London NW5 2BJ, UK

Bd Ediciones de Diseño SA
291 Mallorca, 08037 Barcelona, Spain

OUTLETS
Austria/Germany
IMD Inter Marketing Distribution AG,
Flöthbruchstrasse 11, 4156 Willich 2,
Anrath, Germany

Belgium
Quattro, 25 rue de la Regence, 1000 Brussels

Canada
Triede, 460 McGill, Montreal, Quebec
H2Y 2H2

France
8 rue des Quatre Fils, 75003 Paris

Greece
Varangis Avepe SA, 40 M Botsari,
GR 15121 Pefki

Holland
IMD Inter Marketing Distribution AG,
Beverweerdlaan 22, 6825 AE Arnhem

Hong Kong
Le Cadre Gallery, 8 Sunning Road G/F,
Causeway Bay

Italy
Zoltan, Via Alesandria 5, 20144 Milan

Japan
Art Front Gallery, Daikanyama Edge 3F, 28-10
Sarugaku-cho, Shibuya-ku, Tokyo

Portugal
Arquitectonica, Rua da Escola Politécnica 94,
1200 Lisbon

Singapore
Galeria Ecletique, 58 Tanjong Pagar Road

Switzerland
IMD Inter Marketing Distribution AG,
Eebrunnestrasse 26, 5212 Hausen (AG)

UK
Interior Marketing, 2 Woods Cottages, Hartfield Broad Oak, Bishop's Stortford, Herts. CM22 7BU

USA
Luminaire, 7300 Southwest 45th Street, Miami, Florida 33155; Current, 1201 Wester Avenue, Seattle, Washington 98101; Di-zin, 1320 Main Street, Venice, California 90291

Leonor Bedel & Asociados
Av. Garay 325, 4to 7mo, 1153 Buenos Aires, Argentina

Belux AG
Bremgarterstrasse 109, Wohlen 5610, Switzerland

OUTLETS

Australia
Création Baumann, 87 King William Street, Fitzroy, Victoria 3065

Benelux
Belux Benelux BV, Hettenheuvelweg 14, NL-1101 BN Amsterdam

Canada
Création Baumann, 302 King Street, East Toronto, Ontario M5A 1K6

Czechoslovakia
Sirius Light, Masarykovo Nabrezi 20, CR 11000 Prague 1

Denmark
Osterby Christian, Birkewaenget 21, 3520 Farum

France
Technopolis 4, ZAC de Mercières, 60200 Compiègne

Germany
Nils Holger Moormann, Kirchplatz, 83229 Aschau im Chiemgau

Israel
Belux Israel, Swiss Art Puzzle, Modular Furniture System Ltd, Dizengoffstreet 264, 63117 Tel Aviv

Italy
Piramide s.a.s, Via Feltre 148, 32100 Belluno

Japan
Création Baumann Japan Ltd, Tokyo Design Centre, 5-25-19 Higashi-Gotanda, Shinagawa-ku, Tokyo 141

UK
Lumino Ltd, Lovet Road, Harlow, Essex CM19 5T8

USA
Ernest Stöcklin, 135 Fort Lee Road, Leonia, New Jersey 07605

A. Bianchi srl
Via Salomone No. 41 , Milan 20138, Italy

Blauet
Aragon 333, 09009 Barcelona, Spain

OUTLETS

Denmark
Chr. Osterby, Birkevaenget 21, 3520 Farun

France
Deka Distribution-MME Marceau, 2 bis rue Leon Blun, 91120 Paliseau

Germany
Mary-The Gaya Schüller, Engelbert Strasse 16-26, 50674, Cologne

Greece
Nikos Soulakis, Pablou 9, 54621 Thessaloniki

Holland
Indoor, Paulus Potterstraat 22–24, 1071 DA Amsterdam

Hong Kong
Leo's Collection Ltd, 149 Wongneichong Road G/F, Happy Valley

Italy
Muriel Roland, Via Bocaccio 14, Milan 201234

Japan
Taki In, 11–10 Harchobori 4-chome, Chuo-ku, Tokyo 104

Portugal
Of. Gerais de Desenhos Ind. LDA, R. de Belmonte 97, 4000 Porto

South Africa
Lights by Linea, 9 Bree Street, 8001 Cape Town

Switzerland
Goffredo Loertscher AG, Ringstrasse 13, 4123 Allschwill 1

Taiwan
Furniture Tony, No. 287 Hing Shen W. Rd, 060 Taipei

USA
Estiluz Inc., 211 Gates Road, S.P. Little Ferry, New Jersey, NJ 07643

B.Lux SA
Poligono Eitua s/n, Berriz 48240, Vizcaya, Spain

OUTLETS

Australia
Inlite Pty Ltd, 76–78 Balmain Street, 3121 Richmond

Austria
Plan Licht, Vomperbach 187A, A-6130 Schwaz

Belgium
Boon Agencies, Mechelsestenweg 221, B-3500 Lier

Denmark
Pasta Lab International, Duevej 54, 2000 Copenhagen

Finland
Inno Interior KY, Merikatu 1, 00140 Helsinki

France
Luci France, 96 Bd. Auguste Blanqui, 75013 Paris

Germany
B. Lux Deutschland GmbH, Tulbeckstrasse 55, 8000 Munich 2

Hong Kong
Krohn Ltd, 69 Jervois Street, Mezz Floor

Israel
Alkabes Industries Ltd, 45 Kibutz Galuyot St, 66550 Tel Aviv

Italy
Contempora Di Zannier Luigi, Piazza Rizzolatti 4, Clauzetto 33090

Portugal
Parisete Moveis E Decoracoes, Avenida de Paris 7-A, 1000 Lisbon

Singapore
X.Tra Designs Private Ltd, 236 Tanjong Katong Road, 1543 Singapore

South Africa
Peter Stuart, PO Box 782962-2146 Sandton

Switzerland
Dedalus, Via Gismonda 17, CH-6850 Mendrisio

Taiwan
Pinhole International, No.11 Lane 639, Min Sheng E. Road, 10447 Taipei

UK
Candell Ltd, Carrera House, 33 South Road, London E17 6BH

USA
Artup Corporation, 3101 Shannon Street, Santa Ana, California 92704

Vittorio Bonacina & Co.
Via Madonnina 12, Lurago d'Erba 22040, Como, Italy

Box Products Ltd
Unit 6–8, Bishop's Wharf, 39–49 Parkgate Road, London SW11 4PL, UK

John Bradley Associates
Studio 4, Pickfords Wharf, Clink Street, London SE1 9DG, UK

Maurice Brill
3rd Floor, 3 Swan Field Court, 48 Chilton Street, London E2 6DZ, UK

Brossier Saderne
16 rue du Port de l'Ancre, Angers 49100, France

Catellani & Smith srl
Via Locatelli 47, Villa di Serio 24020, Bergamo, Italy

Cini & Nils srl
Via Francesco Ferrucio 8, Milan 20145, Italy

OUTLETS

Austria
Jandl Wohnbedarf, Boltzmanngasse 12, Vienna

Belgium/Luxembourg
Sig. Hugo Vleminckx (societa Rayo), O.L. Vrouwstraat 78, Mechelen

Germany
(postal districts 1/2/3): Klaus Siemensen, Segeberger Strasse 127, Neumunster; (postal districts 4/5): Klaus Jansen, Stuting Strasse 63, Gevelsberg; (postal districts 6/7/8): Folker Jahnke, Schertlinstrasse 20, Schondorf

Holland
Sig. ra. Hansje Kalff, Puttensestraat 8, Amstelveen

Spain
Sig. Higueras (societa Bedre), Paseo Colon 102–104, Cardedeu, Barcelona

Switzerland
Signora Catherine Corremans (Societa Ipso Facto), 6 rue Joseph Girard, Geneva

Concord Lighting Ltd
174 High Holborn, London WC1V 7AA, UK

OUTLETS

Australia
Sylvania Lighting International, Sylvania Way, Lisarow Box 450, Gosford, New South Wales 2250

Austria
Sylvania Ges.mbH, Postfach 28, Am Sachsengang, 2301 Gross Ezersdorf

Belgium
Sylvania NV, Cross Roads Park, Wezembeekstraat 2, 1930 Zaventem

Brazil
Sylvania do Brasil Iluminacoa Ltd, Rua Amoipra No. 81, 04689-900 Sao Paulo

Costa Rica
Sylvania Costa Rica, San Jose 100, PO Box 1130

Denmark
Sylvania A/S, Jemholmen 38, 2650 Hvidovre

Finland
Sylvania Luminance OY, Sirrikuja 3A, 00940 Helsinki

France
S L I France, Tour Neptune, 20 Place De Seine, Courbevoie Cedex 20, 92086 Paris

Germany
S L I Lichtsysteme GmbH, Graf Zeppelin Strasse 9–11, D-91056 Erlangen

Italy
Tecnolyte SpA, Via Nazionale 193, Rome 00184

Japan
Light Cube Ltd, 1-2 Shiba, 5-chome, Minato-ku, Tokyo

The Netherlands
Luminance BV, Oudeweg 155, 2031 HH Haarlem

Norway
Luminance Norge AS, POB 1129 Lura, N-4301 Sandnes

Portugal
Sylvania Electronica LDA, Zona Industrial, da Barruncheira, Lote a. Apartado 69, Carmaxide, 2795 Linda-A-Velha

Spain
Sylvania SA, Los Llanos de Jerez 17, Poligono Industrial 28820, Coslada, Madrid

Sweden
Sylvania AB, Tellusborgsvagen 94A, Box 32059, 12611 Stockholm

Switzerland
Sylvania SA, 20 Route de Pré Bois, Case Postale 554, 1215 Geneva 15

Taiwan
Taiwan Liaison Office, 11F4 No.230, Jen-Al Road Sec 4, Taipei

Thailand
Thailand Branch, SNC Tower, 5th Floor, 33 Sukhumvit 4, Sukhumvit Road, Bangkok 10110

USA
Sylvania Lighting Intl, Latin American HQ, 6600 N. Andrews Avenue, Suite 240, Fort Lauderdale, Florida 33309

Daiko
Tokyo Office, 4-31-17 Ryogoku, Sumida-ku, Tokyo 130, Japan

OUTLET

Italy
Daiko Euro Liaison Office, Via Vittorio Veneto 5, Marcon 30020, Venice

Dansk Lights Inc.
1224 NE 8th Avenue, Fort Lauderdale, Florida 33304, USA

Ross De Alessi Lighting Design
2815 Second Avenue, Suite 280, Seattle, Washington 98121, USA

David D'Imperio
2961 Aviation Avenue, Miami, Florida 33133, USA

di'(sain) Hagn & Kubala OEG
69 Zieglergasse, Vienna 1070, Austria

Ecart SA
111 rue Saint-Antoine, 75004 Paris, France

Elliott & Associates Architects
35 Harrison Avenue, Oklahoma City, Oklahoma 73104, USA

Equation Lighting Design Ltd
7 Pall Mall Deposit, 124–128 Barlby Road, London W10 6BL, UK

Erco Leuchten GmbH
80–82 Brockhauser Weg, 58507 Lüdenscheid, Germany

OUTLETS

Australia
Spectra Lighting pty, Ltd, 15 Industrial Avenue, Wacol, Queensland 4076

Austria
Erco Leuchten GmbH, Zweigniederlassung Wien, Modeceter Strasse 14/4, OG/BC A-1030, Vienna

Belgium
Erco Lighting Belgium BVDA/SPRL, avenue Molière 211, B-1060 Brussels

Cyprus
J.N. Christofides Trading Ltd, PO Box 1093, 29a Michalakopoulou Str., Nicosia

Denmark
Lightmakers AS, Indiavej 1, Sondre Frihavn 2100, Kobenhavn

Finland
OY Hedengren AB, Lauttasaarentie 50, SF-00 200 Helsinki, Postilokero 190

France
ERCO Lumières sarl, 6ter rue des Saints Pères, 75007 Paris; Succursale Lyon, 4 rue V. Lagrange, 69007 Lyon

Greece
Christos Vakirtzis, Rizari 17, Athens 11634

Hong Kong
Architectural Lighting (HK) Ltd, 3/F Sing Dao Industrial Building, 232 Aberdeen Main Road, Aberdeen

Iceland
Segull Ltd, Eyjaslod 7, IS-101 Reykjavik

Ireland
Erco Lighting Ireland Ltd, 289 Harolds Cross Road, Dublin 6

Italy
Erco Illuminazione, Via Cassanese 224, Palazzo Leonardo, Segrate 20090, Milan

Japan
Erco TOTO Ltd, 3-44-1 Mukoujima, Sumida-ku, J-131 Tokyo

Korea
Alto Co. Ltd, 2nd Floor Tau Seung Bldg, 618–4, Sin sa-Dong, Kang Nam-ku, Seoul

Malaysia
Seng Hup Electric Co. Snd Bhd, 44–2 et 44–3 Jalan Sultan Ismail, 50250 Kuala Lumpur

The Netherlands
Erco Lighting Nederland BV, Goolmeer 13, 1411 De Naarden

Norway
Erco Belysning AS, Industriveien 8 B, 1473 Skarer; Postboks 83, Ellingsrudasen, 1006 Oslo 10

Oman
Delta Ltd, PO Box 4537, Ruwi

Portugal
Omnicel Tecnicas de Illuminaçáo SA, rua Castillo, 57–5. Dto. 1200 Lisbon

Qatar
Rafco, PO Box 831, Old Rayyan Road, Doha

Saudi Arabia
Technolight, PO Box 12679, Jeddah 21483

Singapore
De De Ce Design Centre, c/o Kliktube Electrical Systems Pte Ltd, 121 Keppel Road, Singapore 0409

Spain
Erco Illuminacion SA, Poligono El Pla, c/El Pla s/n (Parcela 28), E-08750 Molins de Rei

Sweden
Aneta Belysning AB, Box 3064, 35033 Växjö

Switzerland
Neuco AG, Würzgrabenstrasse 5, 8048 Zurich

Thailand
Palicon, Pro-Art Lighting Ltd, 4th Floor, 29–4 Sukhumvit 31, Phrakanong, Bangkok 10110

Turkey
Total Aydinlatma Mümessillik, Sanayi ve Ticaret AS, Tevukiye Caddesi No. 73/3, 80200 Istanbul

United Arab Emirates
Scientechnic, PO Box 325, Dubai

UK
Erco Lighting Ltd, 38 Dover Street, London W1X 3RB

Fantasy for Light
Via Marconi, Suisio 24040, Bergamo, Italy

Feldmann & Schultchen
53c Peutestrasse, Hamburg 20539, Germany

Fisher Marantz Renfro Stone Architectural Lighting Design
126 Fifth Avenue, New York, NY 10011, USA

Flos SpA
Via Angelo Faini 2, Bovezzo, Brescia 25073, Italy

OUTLETS
Belgium
Flos SA, Gossetlaan 50, 1720 Groot Bijgaarden
France
France Flos sarl, 5 rue de Bicêtre, 94240 L'Hay Les Roses
Germany
Deutschland Flos GmbH, Am Probsthof 94, 53121 Bonn
Japan
Flos Co. Ltd, PMC Building, 1-23-5 Higashi-Azabu, Minato-ku, Tokyo 106
Spain
Flos SA, c/Bovedillas 16, San Just Desvern, 08960 Barcelona
Switzerland
Flos SA, 75 Blvd St-Georges, 1025 Geneva
UK
Flos Ltd, 31 Lisson Grove, London NW1 6UB
USA
Flos Inc., 200 McKay Road, Huntington Station, New York, NY 11746

Foscarini Murano SpA
1 Fondamenta Manin, Murano, Venice 30141, Italy

OUTLETS
Canada
Agences Volt., 68 rue Alie Dollard Des Ormeaux, Quebec, H9A 1H1
France/Holland
Horas International, 22 rue Copernic Copernicusstraat, B-1180 Brussels
Germany
Altalinea GmbH, Sandhof 6, 41469 Neuss-Norf
Taiwan
H.N. Lin Enterprise Co. Ltd, 32 Chin Shan S. Rd Sec 1, Taipei, R.O.C.
UK
Catalytico Ltd, 25 Montpellier Street, London SW7 1HF
USA
Italiana Luce USA Inc., 400 Long Beach Blvd, Stratford, Connecticut 06497

Kazuko Fujie
B-3F Hillside Terrace Annex, 30–2 Sarugaku-cho, Shibuya-ku, Tokyo 150, Japan

Gallegos Lighting Design
8132 Andasol Avenue, Northridge, California 91325, USA

The Gallery Mourmans
Keizer Karelplein 8B, 6211 TC, Maastricht, The Netherlands/Zeedijk-Zoute 739, 8300 Knokke-Heist, Belgium

Garcia Garay SL
13 San Antonio, Sta Coloma Gramenet 08923, Barcelona, Spain

OUTLETS
Austria
Plan Licht, Fiecht Au 25, Vomp A-6130
Belgium
Elec Lighting NV/SA, Battelsesteenweg 28–34, 2800 Mechelen
France
Inedit SB, 5 rue Charonne, 75011 Paris
Germany
Mega Licht, Breslauer Strasse 14, 63452 Hanua
Holland
Asint Light BV, Montageweg 22, 3433 NT Nieuwegein
Hong Kong
Metalux Collection, Rm 1301, Fook Lee Comm. Centre, Town Place, 33 Lockhart Road
Portugal
Osvaldo Matos Lda, Rua Sta. Barbara 27a 45, Coimbroes, 4400 VN Gaia
Switzerland
G.G. Sparlight AG, Moosstrasse 2, CH-6003 Lucerne
UK
Into Lighting Design Ltd, 2 St Georges Court, Putney Bridge Road, London SW15 2PA

Gargot Disseny Mediterani SA
Pol. Ind. 'Can Sedo', s/n Puig I Llagostera, Esparreguera 08292, Barcelona, Spain

Tobias Grau KG GmbH & Co.
18 Borselstrasse, Hamburg 22765, Germany

Paul Gregory, Focus Lighting Inc.
255 West 101st Street, New York, NY 10025, USA

Guardí
2–4 Katharinengasse, Vienna 1100, Austria

OUTLETS
Germany
Fa. Orbesa, Bürgelin 164, 88090 Immenstaad Bodensee
Italy
Uno-Distributione, Via Cavour 7, Turin 10123

Ashley Hall
9 Legard Road, London N5 1DE, UK

Maria Christina Hamel
Via Tadino 15, Milan 20124, Italy

Inflate
11–13 Corsham Street, London N1 6DP, UK

OUTLETS
Belgium
Luc de Buyser, Langestraat 40, 9160 Lokeren
France
Pachyderme, 11 Av. Simon Bolivar, 75018 Paris

Germany
Jürgen J. Burk, Bucher Strasse 19, 90419 Nürnberg

Irideon Ltd
20–22 Fairway Drive, Greenford, Middlesex UB6 8PW, UK

OUTLETS
Asia
Vari-Lite Asia Inc., Kamino II Building, 1-20-7 Higashi-Gotanda, Shinagawa-ku, Tokyo 141, Japan
USA
Irideon Inc., 201 Regal Row, Dallas, Texas 75247

Masafumi Katsukawa
Via Marchesi de Taddei 18, Milan 20146, Italy

Yasuo Kondo Design Office
T-3 2F Bond Street, 2-2-43 Higashinagawa, Shinagawa-ku, Tokyo, Japan

Koziol GmbH
90 W.V. Siemens Strasse, Erbach 64711, Germany

OUTLETS
Belgium
Zet BVBA, 98 Noorderlaan, Antwerp 2030
France
Vesa, 14 Allée des Fongères, Paris 93340
Italy
Anteprima srl, Via Fonseca Pimentel 11/7, Milan 20127
Japan
Shimada Internati Ing., 15F Canal Tower, Tokyo 103
The Netherlands
Copi, 24B Stadhouderskade, Amsterdam 1054 ES
Scandinavia
Lisbeth Dahl, 8B Harmsdorthsvej, Frederiksberg 1874
Spain
Pilma Disseny SA, 20 Valencia, Barcelona 08015
Switzerland
Samei AG, 16 Oberdorf Strasse, Wadenswil 8820
UK
Environment, 120 High Street, Leeds LS25 5AG
USA
Robert Greenfield Ltd, 225 Fifth Avenue, New York, NY 10010

Kwau Shau An
2-25-16 Horikiri, Katsushika 124, Tokyo, Japan

Danny Lane
19 Hythe Road, London NW10 6RT, UK

New Leucos SpA
Via Treviso 77, Scorze 30037, Venice, Italy

OUTLETS
Austria
Manfred Prunnbauer, Selzergasse 10, 1150 Vienna

France
C & D Diffusion sarl, 23 Rue de Savoie, Immoble Le Boccard, 74704 Sallanches

Germany
Leucos Deutschland GmbH, Bunsenstrasse 5, Martinsried, B. Munich 8033

Japan
Yamagiwa Lighting Centre, 4F, 4-5-18 Higashi-nippori, Arakawa-ku, Tokyo 116

UK
MW United Ltd, 3 Willow Business, London SE26 4QP

USA
Leucos USA Inc., 70 Campus Plaza, Edison, New Jersey 08837

Lighting Design Limited
Lighting Design House, Zero Ellaline Road, London W6 9NZ, UK

Lighting Design Partnership Ltd
63 Gee Street, London EC1V 3RS, UK

Luceplan SpA.
Via E. T. Moneta 44/46, Milan 20161, Italy

OUTLETS
Australia/Singapore
Ke-Zu Pty Ltd, 95 Beattie Street, Balmain, New South Wales 2041

Austria
Lindmaier Möbel & Leuchten, Silbergasse 6, 1190 Vienna

Belgium
Sisterco SA/NV, Altenaken 11, 3320 Hoegaarden

Brazil
Broadway Ind Coms S, Rua des Crisandalias 104, Jardim das Acacias, São Paulo, CEP 04704-020

Denmark
Finn Sloth APS, Heilsmindevej 1, 2920 Charlottenlund

France
Arelux, Zac Paris Nord II, 13 rue de la Perdrix, 93290 Tremblay-en-France

Germany
Agentur Holger Werner GmbH, Nachtigallenweg 1c, D-61462 Koenigstein/TS (postal districts 1,4,5,6,); Doris Schmidt Agentur für Licht und Möbeldesign, Johannesweg 1, D-33803 Steinhagen (postal districts 2,3); Karo – Robert Karl, Amalienstrasse 69, D-80799 Munich

Hong Kong
Artemide Ltd, 102–103 Ruttonjee Centre, 11 Duddell Street

Israel
D.I. Lighting Fixtures Ltd, Heh B'Iyar 22, PO Box 21330, Il-61213 Tel Aviv

Japan
Casa Luce Inc., 3-16-12 Sotokanda, Chiyoda-ku, Tokyo 101

Mexico
Grupo D.I. S de R.L., Altavista 119, Col San Angel, Mexico DF 010160

The Netherlands
Simon Eikelenboom BV, Keomembergweg 54, 1101 GC Amsterdam ZO

Spain
Rotger, C/Nou 8, 08870 Garraf, Barcelona

Sweden
Annell Lluis & Forum AB, Surbrunnsgatan 14, 11421 Stockholm

Switzerland
Andome Engros, Eigentalstrasse 17, 8425 Oberembrach

USA
Luceplan, 900 Broadway No. 902, New York, NY 10003

Lucitalia SpA
Via Pelizza da Volpedo 50, Cinisello Balsamo 20092, Milan, Italy

OUTLETS
Argentina
Luz y Color srl, Sarmiento 1164, 1041 Buenos Aires

Asia
Casa Luce Inc., 3-16-12 Sotokanda, Chiyoda-ku, Tokyo 101

Austria/Germany
Luci Leuchten GmbH, Bürglen 16, 88090 Immenstaad/Bodensee, Germany

Benelux
Quattro Benelux SA, Altenaken 11, 3320 Hoegaarden, Belgium

Canada
Scangift, 821 Tecumseh Road, Pointe Claire, Quebec H9R 4X8

Denmark
Taifo Buying Agencies A/S, Studsgade 35, Box 220, 8100 Aarhus

France
Luxo France SA, 96 Bd Auguste Blanqui, 75013 Paris

Iceland
Heimsljòs, Kringlan 8–12, Reykjavik 103

Israel
Y. Wallisch Technologies Ltd, 7 Kehilat Saloniky St., 69513 Tel Aviv

Italy
Showroom and Projects Development, Lucitalia, Via Brera 30, 20121 Milan

Lebanon
Memas sarl, Dora Gate, Beirut

Switzerland
Gatto Diffusion, rue des Chavannes 30, 2016 Cortaillod

USA
Illuminating Experience Inc., 233 Cleveland Avenue, Highland Park, New Jersey 08904

Venezuela
Lamparas Diana Dos SA, Av. 4 de Majo, Isle Margarita Porlamar

Lumen Centre Italia srl
Via Dina Galli 14, Buccinasco 20090, Milan, Italy

Luxo Italiana SpA
Via della More 1, Presezzo 24030, Bergamo, Italy

OUTLETS
Austria
Ing. Manfred Prunnbauer, Selzergasse 10, Vienna 1150

Belgium
Elma Obreg, Avenue Carton de Wjartlaan, Brussels 1090

Denmark
Luxo Danmark, 27–29 Tempovej, 2750 Ballerup

Finland
Sahkokonsultti Oy, 44B Vihertie, Vantaa 01620

France
Luxo France, 96 Bd Auguste Blanqui, Paris 75013

Germany
Luci Leuchten, 16 Burglen, Immenstaad 68087

Japan
Yamagiwa Corporation, 1-8-18 Shinden, Adachi-ku, Tokyo 123

The Netherlands
Ansems Industrial Design, 10A Dorpsstraat, Ledeacker 58416

Norway
Luxo Norway, 117 Enebakkvn, Manglerud, Oslo

Portugal
Casa das Lampadas Ltda, 894 Rua do Arroteia, Leca do Balio 4465

Spain
Luxo Espanola, 39–41 Sugranyles, Barcelona 0812

Sweden
Luxo Sweden, 10/A Kraketorpsgatan, 43153 Mölndal

UK
Luxo UK Ltd, 4 Barmeston Road, Catford, London SE3 6BN

USA
Zelco Industries Inc., 630 S. Columbus Avenue, Mt Vernon, New York 10550; Luxo Lamp Corporation, 36 Midland Avenue, Port Chester, New York

Marlin
Hanworth Trading Estate, Hampton Road, West Feltham, UK

Ingo Maurer GmbH
47 Kaiserstrasse, 80801 Munich, Germany

OUTLETS
France
Altras sarl, 24 rue Laffitte, 75009 Paris

Japan
Studio Noi Co. Ltd, Rangee Aoyama Bldg, No. 710, 1-4-1 Kita-Aoyama, Minato-ku, Tokyo 107

186

Suppliers

The Netherlands
Inter Collections BV, 2 Bosrand, Schiedam 3121 XA

Scandinavia
Mr Finn Sloth, 1 Heilsmindevej, DK 2920 Charlottenlund, Denmark

Spain
Santa & Cole, 71 Balmes, 08440 Carcedeu, Barcelona

Mazzei SpA
Via Livornese-Est 108, Perignano 56030, Pisa, Italy

Mark McDonnell
7 Russell Avenue, Kentfield, California 94904, USA

Megalit
c/o Artemide GB Ltd, 323 City Road, London EC1V 1LJ, UK

Memphis Milano
Via Olivetti 9, Pregnana Milanese 20010, Milan, Italy

Minerva Co. Ltd.
1-10-7 Hiratsuka, Tokyo 142, Japan

Mito
Via Lamia S.S 18, Nocera Superiore 84015, Salerno, Italy

OUTLETS
Australia
Studio Italia Pty Ltd, 176 Coventry Street, 3205 Victoria, South Melbourne

Austria/Germany
SRS Design Marketing, Steiweg 14, 88299 Leutkirch-Unterzeil

Belux
Carla Doesburg BVBA, Langerstraat 20, 9150 Kruibeke, Belgium

France
New Model sarl, Lou Calendal 12, 13580 La Fare les Oliviers

Greece
Business Design Group, 4/10 Patmou Street, 15123 Maroussi, Athens

Holland
Trampoluce, Archterstraat 12, AZ Den Hout

Korea
Daewon Cable Ltd, Mito Trading, 2 Dong, Songpa-ku, Seoul

Orient
Atalia, Via Disbino 4, 22063 Cantù, Como

Portugal
Arquitectonica LDA, Rua Escola Politecnica 94, 1200 Lisbon

Spain
Hustadt Illuminacion SA, C. Bolivia, 340 Local 60, Barcelona

Switzerland
Riediffusion, avenue Temple 19/c, 1010 Lausanne 10

UK
Eurolights, 655 Finchley Road, London NW2 2HN

USA
Ernest Stoecklin, 135 Fort Lee Road, Leonia, New Jersey 07605

Torsten Neeland
Brahmsallee 19, 20144 Hamburg, Germany

Nordlight SpA (division of Neofos)
Statale Aretina 29/N, Sieci 50069, Florence, Italy

OUTLETS
Belgium
C.I.R. SA, rue J.B. Decock 99/101, 1080 Brussels

Germany
Ticinelli Lichtprojekte, Neuweg 1, 64521 Gross – Gerau

Japan
Japan Camber, 6-16-41 Higashi Ohizumi, Nerima-ku, Tokyo 178

The Netherlands
Asint BV, Montageweg 22, NT 3433 Nieuwegein

UK
Forma Lighting Ltd, Mitcham Industrial Estate, 85 Stratham Road, Mitcham, Surrey CR4 2AP

Noto – Zeus
Corso San Gottardo 21/9, Milan 20136, Italy

OUTLETS
France
Gilles Chennouf, 15 Rue du Petit Musc, 75004 Paris

Germany
Sabine Hainlen, Hermann Kurz Strasse 14, 7000 Stuttgart

Japan
Ambiente Int., 4-11-1 Minami Aoyama, Minato-ku, Tokyo 107

The Netherlands
Miracles, 218 Prinsengracht, 1018, Amsterdam

UK
Viaduct Furniture Ltd, 1–10 Summer's Street, London EC1R 5BD

USA
Luminaire, 7300 S.W. 45th Street, Miami, Florida 33155

Oceano Oltreluce
Via Tortona 14, Milan 20144, Italy

O Luce
Via Conservatorio 22, Milan 20122, Italy

Dominique Perrault Architecte
26/34 rue Bruneseau, 75013 Paris, France

Louis Poulsen & C. A/S
11 Nyhavn, DK-1001 Copenhagen K, Denmark

OUTLETS
Australia
Louis Poulsen Lightmakers Pty Ltd, 755–759 Botany Road, Roseberry, New South Wales 2018

Finland
Louis Poulsen OY, Kanavaranta 3 D 9, SF 00160 Helsinki

France
Louis Poulsen & Cie sarl, 128 bis avenue Jean Jaures, F-94851 Ivry sur Seine, Cedex

Germany
Louis Poulsen & Co. GmbH, Postfach 1563, D-42379 Haan

Holland
Louis Poulsen BV, Paredlaan 26, 2132 WS Hoofddorp

Japan
Loius Poulsen Japan KK, 2-11-13 Higashiazabu, Minato-ku, Tokyo 106

Norway
Louis Poulsen & Co. A/S, Lilleakerveien 2, Boks 102, Lilleaker, N-0216 Oslo 2

Sweden
Louis Poulsen AB, Neue Winterthurerstrasse 28, CH-8304 Wallisellen–Zurich

USA
Poulsen Lighting Inc., 5407 N.W. 163 Street, Miami, Florida 33014-6130

Prandina srl
Via Capitelvecchio 5, Bassano del Grappa 36061, Vicenza, Italy

OUTLETS
Germany and Benelux
Prandina BV, De Koumen 86, NL 06433 KE Heerlen

Portugal
Lancari, Rua do Campo Alegre, 1380 HAB 124, Porto

Spain
Kambi Iluminacion, Blay Net, 35 A. de Correos, E-08830 Sant Boi de LL., Barcelona

USA
Current, 1201 Western Avenue, Seattle, Washington, USA

Quattrifolio srl
Via Ferraris 19–21, Cusago 20090, Milan, Italy

OUTLET
UK
gfc Lighting Ltd, Westminster Business Square, Durham Street, London SE11 5JA

Karim Rashid
145 W. 27th Street, 4E, New York, NY 10001, USA

Sarah Reilly
Workshop B10, Faircharm Trading Estate, 8–12 Creekside, Deptford, London SE8 3DX, UK

OUTLET
Japan
HOF Lighting, No. 100 Sec. 3, Jen Ai Road, Taipei, Taiwan, R.O.C.

Sakeagi Design Studio
1–74 Nakamizuno-cho, Seto-shi 489, Aichi-ken, Japan

Santa & Cole Ediciones de Diseño SA
10 Santisima Trinidad del Monte, Barcelona 0817, Spain

OUTLETS
Germany
Triforma, Adolf Sandbergerstrasse 8, 81243 Munich

Hong Kong
Apartment, 940 Tung Lo Wan Road, 9th Floor, Causeway Bay

Italy
Eleber, Corso San Felice 50, Vicenza 36100

Japan
Annick Ass., 101–9 Meguro 18, 4-chome, Meguro KV, Tokyo 153

UK
London Lighting, 133–135 Fulham Road, London SW3 6RT

USA
Modern Living, 8125 Melrose Avenue, Los Angeles, California 90046

Schuler & Shook Inc.
213 West Institute Place, Suite 610, Chicago, Illinois 60610, USA

Sirrah srl gruppo iGuzzini
Via Molino Rosso 8, Imola 40026, Bologna, Italy

OUTLETS
Australia
E.C.C. Lighting, 18–20 Allen Street, Pyrmont, New South Wales 2009

Germany
iGuzzini Illuminazione Deutschland GmbH, Bunsenstrasse 5, 82152 Planegg

Singapore
Relex Electric (F.E.) Pte Ltd, 605a Marpherson Road, 08–04 Citonac Industrial Complex, Singapore 1336

UK
iGuzzini Illuminazione UK Ltd, Unit 3, Mitcham Industrial Estate, 85 Streatham Road, Mitcham, Surrey CR4 2AP

USA
Illuminating Experiences, 233 Cleveland Avenue, Highland Park, 08904 New Jersey

SKK Lighting
34 Lexington Street, London W1R 3HR, UK

SLAMP (division of Samuel Parker)
Via Bolivia 16, Pomezia 00040, Rome, Italy

OUTLETS
Austria
Emiliano Agentour International, Viktorgasse 12/5a, 1040 Vienna

Belgium
Thema Design, Rue Cogge Straat 16–24, 01210 Brussels

Germany
LIPS GmbH, Werner Heisenberg Strasse 27, 46446 Emmerich

Greece
Anson Antoniadis, 24–26 Filonos Str., 18531 Piraeus

Spain
Arte Libre, Copernico 28, 08021 Barcelona

Switzerland
Manzelli & Eroyan, Postfach 1572, 05610 Wohlen

Solzi Luce srl
Via del Sale 46, Cremona 26100, Italy

OUTLETS
Germany
Robert, Bunsenstrasse 5, Postfach 1229, 8033 Martinsreed

The Netherlands
Taifo 35, Box 220 Studsgade, Aarhus

UK
GFC, Westminster Business Square, Durham Street, London SE11 5JA

USA
Lighting Bug, 320 West 202 ND, 60411 Chicago Heights

Space
28 All Saints' Road, London W11 1HG, UK

Ayala Sperling-Serfaty
69 Maze'h St., 65789 Tel Aviv, Israel

OUTLETS
Germany/Switzerland/Austria
Gabriele Ammann, Designer's Agency, Prinzregentenstrasse 2, 83022 Rosenheim, Germany

UK
David Gill, 60 Fulham Road, London SW3 6HH

USA
Odegard Inc., 200 Lexington Avenue, Suite 1206, New York, NY 10016

Staff GmbH & Co. KG
Grevenmarschstrasse 74–78, 32657 Lemgo, Germany

OUTLETS
Austria
Zumtobel Licht Ges. mbh, Schweizerstrasse 30, 6851 Dornbirn

Belgium
Elma Obreng NV, Oude Gentweg 100, 2070 Zwijndrecht-Burcht

Denmark
Louis Poulsen & Co. A/S, Sluseholmen SV, 2450 Copenhagen

Finland
Louis Poulsen Oy, Kanavaranta 3D, 00 160 Helsinki

France
Zumtobel-STAFF (France) sarl, B.P. 4, 67127 Molsheim Cedex, Avenue de la Gare, 67120 Duttlenheim

Iceland
Reykjafell GmbH, Skipholti 35, 125 Reykjavik

Ireland
Bob Bushell Ltd, 2 Sir John Rogersons Quay, Dublin 2

Italy
Zumtobel STAFF, Illuminazione srl, Viale Berbera 49, Milan 20162

Luxembourg
ELCO ME SA, 9 rue de la Déportation, 1415 Luxembourg

The Netherlands
Dieter Kuenen, Veronaplein 16, 5237 EH 's Hertogenbosch

Norway
STAFF Belyssning as, Postboks 20 44, Hasle, 3239 Sandefjord

Portugal
Lledo Iluminacao, Portugals Lda, Pua Vitorino Nemesio, 10-C, 1700 Lisbon

Spain
Lledo Iluminacion SA, Apartado de Correos 50331, 28080 Madrid

Sweden
Annell Ljus Och Form AB, Surbrunnsgatan 14, 11421 Stockholm

Switzerland
Zumtobel Licht AG, Riedackerstrasse 7, 8153 Rümlang, Zurich

Turkey
Cedetas, Ciragan Cad. No. 46, 80700 Besiktas, Istanbul

UK
STAFF Lighting Ltd, Unit 5, The Argent Centre, Pump Lane, Hayes, Middlesex UB3 3BL

Status
Via Vittorio Veneto 21–23, Bernate Ticino 20010, Milan, Italy

Stiletto Studios
2 Peterburger Platz, Berlin 10249, Germany

OUTLETS
Austria
Di[sain] Hagn & Kubala OEG, 69 Zieglergasse, Vienna 1070

Targetti Sankey SpA
Via Pratese 164, Florence 50145, Italy

OUTLETS
France
Targetti Sankey SA, 15–16 rue des Marronniers, 94240 L'Hay-les-Roses

Germany
Targetti Licht Vertriebs GmbH, 7/A Zum Eisenhammer, Oberhausen 46049

Spain
Targetti Iluminacion SA, 120 Calle Cromo, Hospitalet de Llobregat, Barcelona

UK
Targetti UK, Suite A, 2nd Floor, 138 South Street, Romford RM1 1TE

USA
Tivoli Industries Inc., 1513 East Street, Gertrude Place, Santa Ana 92705, California

Tre ci Luce
Via per Limbiate 60, Solaro 20020, Milan, Italy

Vanlux SA
Poligono Eitua s/n, Berriz 48240, Vizcaya, Spain

Katrien Van Liefferinge
3rd Floor Design Studios, Unit 6, Carr Mills, 322 Meanwood Road, Leeds LS7 2HY, West Yorkshire, UK

OUTLET
Benelux
Erik Huysmans BVBA/Tekna, Dijkstraat 1A, 9160 Lokeren, Belgium

Venini SpA
50 Fond.ta Vetrai, Murano, Venice 30141, Italy

OUTLETS
France
Collectania, 168 rue de Rivoli, Paris 75001

Germany
Graf Bethusy – Huc Vertriebs, 1 Hans-Sachs-Strasse, Krailling 8033

Hong Kong/Singapore
Lane Crawford Ltd, 28 Tong Chong Street, 8/F Somerset House, Quarry Bay, Hong Kong

Japan
Kitaichi Glass Co. Ltd, 1-6-10 Hanazono, Otaru, Hokkaido 047

Monaco
L'Art Venitien, 4 Avenue de la Madone, Monaco 98000

The Netherlands
Desideri, 50 Gossetlaan, Groot-Bijgaarden 1702, Belgium

Saudi Arabia
Khair M., Al-Khadra Trading Estate, PO Box 1376, Jeddah 21431

UK
Liberty Retail Ltd, Regent Street, London W1R 6AH

USA
Hampstead Lighting & Accessories, Suite 100, 1150 Alpha Drive, Alpharetta, GA 30201

Vetreria de Majo srl
Via Galilei 13/D, Mirano 30035, Italy

Villiers Brothers
Fyfield Hall, Fyfield, Near Ongar, Essex CMS 0SA, UK

Weyers & Borms
Antwerpse Steenweg 48/5, 9140 Tielrode, Belgium

Woka Lamps Vienna
16 Singerstrasse, Vienna 1010, Austria

OUTLETS
Belgium
Scratch sprl, Place Rouppe 18, B-1000 Brussels

France
Altras, 24 rue Laffitte, Paris 75009

Germany
H.H. Bünnagel, 2A Robert Koch Strasse, Köln 41

Hong Kong
Visual Lane, Shop 212, 2/F Caroline Centre, 2–38 Yun Ping Road

Italy
Gabriele Galimberti, Via Ponchielli 44, Monza.20052

Japan
AIDEC, 28 Mori Bldg, Nishiazabu 4, 28 Minato-ku, Tokyo 106

The Netherlands
Art Collection, 63 Weijland, Nieuwerbrug 2415

Spain
B.d Ediciones de Diseño, 291 Mallorca, Barcelona 37

Sweden
IDE Individuell, Basargatan 6, S-41117 Göteborg

Switzerland
Vitrine AG, 73 Gerechtigkeitsgasse, Bern CH-3011

UK
M.W. United Ltd, 84 Great Brownings, London SE21 7ZB

USA
George Kovacs, 67–25 Otto Road, Glendale, New York, NY 11385

Hans Wolff & Partners BV
Herengracht 162, 1016 BP Amsterdam, The Netherlands

Yamada Shoumei
3-16-12 Sotokanda, Chiyoda-ku, Tokyo 101, Japan

Y Design (Leonid Yentus)
130 72nd Street No. 3C, Brooklyn, New York, NY 11209, USA

Zoltan
Via Alessandria 5, Milan 20100, Italy

Zumtobel Licht GmbH.
30 Schweizerstrasse, A-6850 Dornbirn, Austria

OUTLETS
France
Zumtobel – Agence Ile de France, 2 rue de la Cristallerie, 92310 Sèvres

Germany
Zumtobel Licht GmbH, 2–4 Achtzehn-Morgen Weg, 61242 Usingen

Italy
Zumtobel Staff Illuminazione srl, Viale Bervera 49, Milan 20162

Japan
Koizumi Sangyo Corp., 3–12 Kanda-Sakumacho, Chiyoda-ku, Tokyo 101

The Netherlands
N.V. Zumtobel Benelux SA, 14 Cannaertserf, Breda 4824

Scandinavia
Zumtobel Belysning AB, 140 A. Ulvsundavägen, 16130 Bromma, Stockholm

Spain
Lledo Illuminacion SA, 14 Cid Campeador, 28080 Mostoles, Madrid

Switzerland
Zumtobel Licht AG, 7 Riedackerstrasse, 8153 Rümlang

UK
Zumtobel Lighting Systems Ltd, Unit 5, The Argent Centre, Pump Lane, Hayes, Middlesex UB3 3BL

USA
Zumtobel Lighting Inc., 141 Building 16D, Lanza Avenue, 07026 Garfield, New Jersey

Photographic Credits

The publisher and author would like to thank the designers, consultants and manufacturers who submitted work for inclusion; Junko Popham for her help with the Japanese contributions, and the following photographers and copyright holders for the use of their material (page numbers are given in brackets).

Jean B. Aegerter (100 bottom)
Hiroshi Aoki (76 top)
Satoshi Asakawa (14–15)
Bitetto-Chimenti (25 centre and right)
Berner Borchardt (101 bottom right)
Mark Burgin © *Belle* magazine (89 bottom right)
Santi Caleca (22–3 centre)
Licia Cappelli (136 *Mondial*)
Richard Davies (152 top and bottom)
Caren Dissinger (68, 69)
Martin Doyle (72–3 table lamps)
© Georges Fessy (160–1)
Klaus Frahm (44–5)
Ferran Freixa (150, 151)
Patrice Gallegos (9, 112–13)
Doug Hall (97 centre and right)
Steve Hall © Hedrich-Blessing (42, 43)
Barry Hannaford (162–3)
Hans Hansen (140)
© Tony Harris (120–1)
Sebastian Hedgecoe (70, 71)
L. Herreman (104)
Masafumi Katsukawa (62 left, 101 left)
Koen Keppens (105 top right)
Christoph Kicherer (153 top)
William Klein (99 right)
Paul Kozlowski and Henri Torquist (135 *Borealis*)
Chris Lewis (116–17)
© John Edward Linden (148, 149)
© Juan Pablo Liva (110–11)
Mr Manciucca c/o Caffe Studios (62 right)
Carmen Masia (94 left, 95 left, 127 centre)
© Nick Meers (56, 57)
Yoram Mitelstadt (11, 58–9, 78–9, 80, 81 left)
Shigeru Ono (26, 27 left, 54, 55)
Nacasa & Partners Inc. (46–7)
Jean-Pierre Peersman (98, 99 left)
Tommaso Pellegrini (18 *Tina*, 20 top left and right, 21 left)
Philips (52–3)
© Robert Pisano (118–19)
Poligraf (64 top left and bottom)
Alfio Pozzoni (107 right)
Armando Rebatto (88 left)
Dirk Reinartz (8, 50–1)
Barbara Sachers (72 left, 73 right)
Douglas Salin (164–5)
Michele Salmi (74 left)
© Scagliola/Brakkee (114–15)
Jan. Chr. Schultchen (30)
Bob Shimer © Hedrich-Blessing (48, 49)
Luis Steinkellner (39)
Beba Stoppani (82)
Studio Mauro Fabbio (28 top left, 142 bottom)
Symmetrical (84, 85, 102 bottom right)
Tandem, Milan (96 right)
Jason Tozer (61 top left)
Emilio Tremolada (21, 28 bottom right, 92 left and top right)
Tom Vack (36 left, 66, 67 left, 122–3, 128)
Hector and Jorge Verdecchia (158, 159)
© Deidi von Schaewen (108, 109)
Peter Weidlein, North Light Studio (24 left, 28 *Joseph*)
Peter Wood (106 right, 107 left)
Gleb Yentus (83, 86)
Miro Zagnoli (74 centre, 127 bottom left)
Max Zambelli (35 right)
Andrea Zani (20 bottom left, 18–19, 136 bottom right, 137).

Index